"Pamela Smith brings us into and through the lenten season with the wisdom of a contemplative and the insight of a poet. Her book is characterized by an economy of words and a freshness of insight that enable the reader to experience Lent with awe, wonder, and a genuine spirit of renewal.

"Her meditations offer challenges to seek hope out of injustice, love out of emotional instability, nobility out of manipulation, help out of callousness, contentment out of perplexity, and stability out of chaos."

Rev. T. Ronald Haney
Author, *Today's Spirituality: The Jesus Story Revisited*

"In *Days of Dust and Ashes*, Pamela Smith has given us a book to help us conduct our own personal lenten retreat. Her daily reflections for the days of Lent are, as the subtitle asserts, truly a hope-filled summons to us dusty, ash-smudged lenten pilgrims to encounter anew the risen Christ."

Sandra DeGidio, O.S.M.
Author, *Sacraments Alive* and *Prayer Services for the Elderly*

"Pamela Smith reaches deep inside herself in these lenten meditations and gifts the reader with her reflections on such experiences as living with diabetes, violence and poverty in our cities, AIDS, aging, and the small epiphanies of daily life. All of these are related to the daily scripture readings for the season. Honest, sometimes painfully so, but always hopeful, Pamela Smith is a welcome companion for the lenten journey. Her book allows us to see more deeply into ourselves, our lives, and our faith."

Susan A. Ross
Theology Department
Loyola University of Chicago

"In this extraordinary work, Dr. Smith presents, in the most exquisite, almost poetic prose, a series of lenten meditations that are brief, challenging, and rich with insight. The combination of theological learning, spiritual depth, and personal sharing she has achieved in crafting these eloquent reflections is itself a testimony of the divine grace she celebrates throughout the work.

"There is nothing particularly pious or sentimental about these meditations. They are often challenging, occasionally hard, frequently moving. Rarely, if ever, have I read a book whose title so accurately captures the book's content. Any author who has the talent and insight to summarize the Lord's Prayer in the simple expression, 'Great God, be our enough' and the good sense to pray in response to that insight, 'So do, Great God, be my enough too,' fully deserves to be read cover to cover. These are meditations suited to a spiritual life in the twenty-first century that can again remind all of us of the need for and significance of the lenten season."

James P. Hanigan, Chair
Theology Department
Duquesne University

"Sr. Pamela Smith draws on both personal experience and the wisdom of many different disciplines to illustrate for the reader the hermeneutic of the scriptural text of the day. The daily reflections elevate the ordinary and reveal the grandeur of God within the everyday 'stuff' of life. She shares her grace-filled encounters with others so that the reader may approach similar encounters with a renewed vision. Each of the daily reflections ends with a short prayer. The prayer written in the first person singular helps the reader to personalize the reflection. This book is a wonderful resource for homilists and homemakers alike. It would be a valuable gift for catechumens and candidates who are journeying through the lenten season towards full communion during the Easter Vigil."

John C. Kemper, S.S.
Associate Professor of Pastoral Theology
SS. Cyril and Methodius Seminary

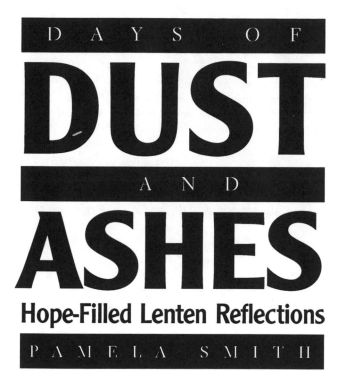

DAYS OF
DUST
AND
ASHES

Hope-Filled Lenten Reflections

PAMELA SMITH

TWENTY-THIRD PUBLICATIONS
Mystic, CT 06355

ACKNOWLEDGMENT

All scriptural quotations are from _The Holy Bible: New Revised Standard Version,_ ©1989, Division of Christian Education of the National Council of the Churches of Christ in the United States of America; published by Oxford University Press, New York.

Twenty-Third Publications
185 Willow Street
P.O. Box 180
Mystic, CT 06355
(860) 536-2611
800-321-0411

ISBN 0-89622-684-0
Library of Congress Catalog Card Number 95-61866
Printed in the U.S.A.

DEDICATION

TO ELNORA WARNER

CONTENTS

INTRODUCTION

One late August morning, as I was hurrying to a learning skills program at Duquesne University, I walked briskly into a freshly washed glass wall that I mistook for a wide-open door. Stunned but stubborn, I backed away, assured two nearby students that I was all right, and headed, with a thumping on the left side of my forehead, toward Canevin Hall. Then I noticed that blood was dripping steadily—on my blouse, on the ground, on the tissues that I rapidly raised to the wound above my eye. The campus chaplain saw me and immediately diagnosed my need for stitches. A maintenance worker called the campus police, and I had an escort to Pittsburgh's Mercy Hospital. The dripping continued, and I noticed, too, that the new glass left lens of my bifocals had a streak that would not wipe off—a long, unpleasant scratch.

The stitching job was perfunctory. It added length and thickness to my eyebrow. For several days I took whatever they had told me to take for pain. I amused myself by making up whacko accounts of the origins of the amazing pink, purple, yellow, olive green, blue, red-violet, violet-blue shiner with which I was beginning a new semester.

What was most memorable about the event was not the kaleidoscopic progress of the black eye, or the permanent scar line established in proximity with my glasses frames, or the bemused expression on the faces of the new students presented with a multiple choice "quiz" on the explanation for my heavily punched appearance on day one of the fall semester. The memorable part was, instead, my encounter with the resident in emergency medicine.

We discovered early on in our conversation that we had in

common our insulin-dependent diabetes. We were on the same two types of insulin (regular and ultra-lente), the same regimen of multiple shots (five a day), a similar pattern of frequent blood tests, and the guesswork of self-managed doses. Both of us had had our miserable days, frightening episodes, frustrations, and fears. The resident admitted to me that he was in emergency medicine because it was sudden, sporadic, varied, and challenging—but also because it preserved him from repeated encounters with diabetics in kidney failure, diabetics gone blind, diabetic amputees who seemed to go nowhere but downhill. I admitted to him that when a service project took a small group of students and me, during my high school teaching years, to a Veterans Administration hospital, I could often only stare at walls and dull myself with television for the remainder of the evening after rounds of visits and feedings. Too many of the debilitated happened to be diabetic. One bedfast man had told me the story of how his medical bracelet had failed to protect him from being jailed for public drunkenness and how the real problem, a severe insulin reaction, had gone quite long untreated—with consequent damages. Like the young doctor, I found that a commitment to an intensive regimen of care and good continuing education in diabetes did not spare me the mix of panic and depression that set in when the bad-case scenarios for my future appeared.

I have been a "brittle" diabetic for more than twenty-five years. The doctor was only a shade older than that himself, but he had been diagnosed with the disease as a preteen. It's a tough and dismal illness, we agreed. Yet he also seemed to take heart at meeting someone who had had the worst form of the disease for so long and still could see, walk four or six miles a day, work without taking more than one sick day in the past five years, enjoy life, write books, have sensation and reflexes in the feet (the first to go), and keep on keeping on. He had a wife, he told me, who understood as well as she could his dietary needs, his routine, the vagaries of the disease, and, to some extent, his inevitable mood swings. Both of us, it appeared, were chronically ill but generally well. We also both preferred not to look too often or too closely at the damages that diabetes mellitus can inflict.

In many ways this chance meeting at Mercy Hospital is a parable of the human condition. Almost all of us, in some spiritual and psycho-emotional sense, can be described as chronically ill but generally well. We have our intractable vices. We have our bad days and our irremediable limits. We would prefer, however, not to confront the possible consequences of our worst tendencies or our worst temptations. We choose not to acknowledge the possibility of dead-end outcomes to any phase of our existence or efforts. We shrink back, hole up, and focus on what we can stand. Every now and then we happen on someone who is afflicted as we are, someone who understands our situation exactly and knows firsthand where and why we run scared.

Meanwhile, we are generally well. We are, for the most part, decent citizens, friends, and spouses. We try to live peaceably and to contribute to good causes. Occasionally we may even champion one. We're not heinous criminals or mortal sinners. There may be a certain lackluster in our character and a certain dissipation or dissoluteness at times in our direction, but we manage to stay substantially on track as we move and age along. All of that notwithstanding, we really would rather, deep down, avoid any specters that might hover, will-o'-the-wisp and spooking, along the roadway.

Lent is a time when we are faced, like it or not, with an opportunity to meet those specters. The wages of sin and the inevitability of death, the flaccidity of the human spirit and the stories of ourselves that we would just as soon not retell, all appear. The season of Lent reminds us of mortality, vulnerability, and moral failure. It hangs a bracelet on us to give notice that we're chronically ill no matter how well we may look or feel or persuade ourselves we are.

The meditations that follow assume our illness and assume that we all possess a measure of health. They speak of suffering that comes our way and suffering we may cause or be implicated in. Each reflection springs from the gospels indicated for the days of Lent in the Roman Catholic lectionary. Each somehow tells a story of our human condition; each takes the viewpoint of "us" in the first person plural. And each is concluded with a first person singular prayer, an "I" statement, which admits complicity in the illness of humankind, invites divine assistance, and yet also acknowledges our potential wholeness, our health, our capacity for grace.

During Lent we recall, no matter how grudgingly, that we are dust and ashes. But during Lent we also meet Someone who knows who we are and comprehends where we cringe and ache. It is that same One who holds out hope. The man of sorrows, the suffering servant, breathes so much life into us that we can be, as Thomas Aquinas has said, both slime and microcosm—and also, as Martin Luther has reiterated, simultaneously sinners and saved.

ASH WEDNESDAY
Matthew 6:1–6, 16–18

"Whenever you pray, go into your room and shut the door and pray to your Father who is in secret; and your Father who sees in secret will reward you."

Matthew 6:6

Every Ash Wednesday, Catholics read this gospel, with its warnings against public displays of piety, and every Ash Wednesday they proceed to go to their offices, factories, schools, and stores visibly smudged with ashes. The contradiction points, at least, to a kind of ongoing tension between the meaningfulness of public "witness" and the necessity of intimate, private prayer. The juxtaposition of the message heard and the ashes worn may also have an element of self-parody about it: an acknowledgment that even on the day when we embark on a hearty return to God we aren't quite sure whether we can live God's word in its simplicity and spareness. We seem to need so many symbols and props.

The bigger question of the gospel doesn't seem, though, to be over the place of public worship and external signs. It seems instead to be this question about the hiddenness, the secrecy, of God. Three times we hear about the Father "who sees in secret" (Matthew 6:4, 6:6, 6:18) and twice about the fact that God somehow *"is* in secret," or (in other translations) "is hidden" (6:6, 6:18).

We have to admit that there is a mystery about every personality, human or divine. No matter how long or how well we have known a friend or loved one, we can still be surprised and mystified by her or him at times. No matter how closely we have looked into ourselves, we can still be startled by our own contradictions. We can be baffled by the emergence of latent vices as well as by the late blooming of certain virtues and gifts. It ought not to be surprising, then, to find out that there are endless inscrutabilities and secrecies about God.

Just as the devotion of private time and quiet time is the only way to get to know a bit more about ourselves and about our friends, it seems that spending time in our inner room with its resolutely shut door is the only way to discover something more of the depths of God. Self-revelation, at its most profound, requires a one-to-one encounter, a heart-to-heart.

This gospel's cautions about almsgiving, prayer, and fasting—the classic disciplines of the penitent—point to the need to shed superficiality, to remove any traces of attention-getting, to eschew mixed motives. The cautions are a call to self-disclosure, the disclosure of some of our own hiddenness. But they are also a guarantee that going to God in intimacy will unveil for us some of God's own secrecy, hiddenness, mystery.

Where, today, are the hideaways where I can hear the beat of your heart? When can I bare my soul before you, O God, and hope to learn, in return, your secrets? I'm looking for the silence and the space, even amid much hubbub.

THURSDAY AFTER ASH WEDNESDAY
Luke 9:22–25

Then he said to them all, "If any want to become my followers, let them deny themselves and take up their cross daily and follow me." Luke 9:23

The prospect of losing life, for those of us who passionately love it, is far from pretty. For those of us who have fought hard for years to keep it—by stiff routines of medication, diet, and exercise—the idea of the final letting-go seems somehow cruel and incomprehensible. Yet the question of the cross may not be altogether about dying. Perhaps it is more about what we live for and how.

Elnora lives in a trailer in the Pocono mountains at the edge of woods where a bear she once nicknamed "Snickers" may still prowl. In her early forties she had to retire from her housekeeping job at a resort because of the accumulated damages of undiagnosed chronic obstructive pulmonary disease and asthma. Heart problems shortly ensued, and so she winds each day's clock around inhalers, pills, nitro patches, and a diet most people would consider unpalatable. On her discouraged days, she wants to live to be one hundred fifty. On better days, when the sun is shining, the cat and dog are playful, the birds are chirping, and paw prints outside the door reveal that a thaw is on, she rekindles her hope to live to see her two hundredth birthday.

For Elnora there can hardly be enough days and hours to notice what new wildflowers have sprung up, what new hymns have been composed, what new discoveries about the Bible have been made, what new sounds have echoed from the next hill. She talks to her pets, to folks on the phone, and to God all day—chiding, praising, complaining, teasing, badgering, sweet-talking (the latter in particular). Her motto might well be summed up in the one claimed by the bishop who lives one diocese away from her: "Love life and do good." She learns sign language so that she can communicate with whatever deaf person she might meet; she prays for people who are healthier than she is; she writes and sends cards to elders and shut-ins. When she speaks of Christ, words like "Rock" and "Savior" don't seem to fit. For her, he is more like a comfortable older brother that one sits with over coffee and donuts. He doesn't have to be polite. If he wants to wear a baseball cap (forwards or backwards) in her house, it's all right.

If taking up her cross means getting through the day with a measure of balance, gratitude, and good cheer, she'll do it. If losing her life for Christ's sake means being consciously and grandiosely sacrificial, she'll hem and haw. If, however, it means doing what comes naturally, being attuned to the rhythms of the day, and keeping up steady conversation with an unseen Friend, then she'll shrug and consent that she's doing at least that. She's had to loosen her grip on life quite a bit, she'll admit, but she's not sitting around thinking about how holy it is to let it ebb away.

If Elnora is "losing her life" for Christ's sake, it's more a matter of doing what she has to do to stay somewhat well, renewing her sense of wonder in everyday creatures and events, deflating puffed-up seriousness with a bit of humor, and trusting that a Power beyond herself is in charge of those more weighty matters of life and death. She doesn't dwell on those ultimates too much, however. There's a vegetable garden to be planned, a card to mail, a dizzy songbird or two to feed, and a sky to be inspected. God is, after all, the God of the living, isn't he (or she)? At nightfall, it makes more sense to Elnora to review how she has lived a full "Yes!" and give thanks than to locate the day's small deaths.

Jesus, brother, help me to walk today, confident of your companionship. Let me shoulder whatever crosses may come with a sense that they are facts of life. And, if I'm preoccupied at all, let it be with lifesigns and love and worldlings around me rather than with the drudgeries of life, prolonging and slow death. Focus me on the good of living, with you alongside.

FRIDAY AFTER ASH WEDNESDAY
Matthew 9:14–15

And Jesus said to them, "The wedding guests cannot mourn as long as the bridegroom is with them, can they? The days will come when the bridegroom is taken away from them, and then they will fast."

Matthew 9:15

What sort of fasting should the happy do? When should those fast for whom the Lord is both present and absent, for whom the reign of God is already here but not yet?

At least two occasions for some fasting seem to present themselves today.

One is the fasting that is the tried and true spiritual discipline, self-imposed, offered up for some good intention, a "mortification" that opens us up to whatever of God we have covered over or crowded out. It can be the quite traditional one full meal and two small "somethings," or it can be even more severe.

Another is the fasting that is undertaken for the sake of justice. It might be a fasting from grapes or lettuce, done in concert with a migrant workers' protest. It might be a fasting from the products of a company that slashes and burns rain forests to graze cattle for hamburgers or runs poor tenants off their patch of farmland to expand pineapple plantations for U. S. marketing. It might be a fasting from coffee or chocolate, because these luxuries have become the cash crops of Third World countries, cultivated because of international debt, often grown at the expense of hungry people who need vegetables, fruit, beans, rice.

Whatever the motive, any fasting we do must be done for solidarity: solidarity of our own souls with the spirit of Christ; solidarity with the poor and the victimized; solidarity with those who are empty, those who are made empty for us.

The one-day Rice Bowl and world hunger fasts are noble but not enough. They raise cash for a soup kitchen here, a relief program there, even as they raise a moment's consciousness. The one-day restraints of Ash Wednesday and Good Friday are respectable communal gestures and symbolic reminders of our own call to repentance, to redirection, and to the total self-emptying of Jesus. But these fasts do not alter the world order or really convert us.

What seems to be our most pressing—and most eagerly avoided—need is to ask what we ought to fast from lastingly, over the long stretch. What fills us so full that it steals the "bridegroom" from our view? What might we need, once and for all, to forgo?

Even now, Lord, I find myself beginning a recitation of reasons why I can't fast, really shouldn't, don't need to. I juggle all these medical dietetics every day. So why shouldn't I go out and eat Chinese? Pizza? Something vegetarian? But that's not the point, is it? What indulgence do I need to shed to clear the way for love of someone in another hemisphere? And also (thus) for you?

SATURDAY AFTER ASH WEDNESDAY
Luke 5:27–32

Jesus answered, "Those who are well have no need of a physician, but those who are sick; I have come to call not the righteous but sinners to repentance."

Luke 5:31-32

None of us really appreciates being considered disabled, deficient, dysfunctional, ill. Yet in some way—obvious or subtle, acute or chronic—every one of us seeks after health and will sometime exhibit extremes in our need for healing. Every one of us will experience some shattering of well-being. All that, in spite of our usual, programmed American response to the question, "How are you?":

"I'm fine!"

"Okay."

"Couldn't be better!"

"Real good. How about you?"

We're always hunky-dory, as far as the general public goes. That's what we want to be—and believe we are expected to be.

We figure that people don't actually want a catalogue of our aches, griefs, self-doubts, daily calamities, irritations, old wounds, upsets, frustrations, cramps, disturbances, fixations, addictions, private miseries when they toss off a jovial "How ya doin'?"

Our best friends may know, and God certainly knows, that we're sometimes just barely "doin'" at all. But we're not all that eager to publicize it, whether to strangers, to intimates, or even to ourselves.

We never really hear whether the "large crowd of tax collectors and others" were miffed when Jesus compared them to "those who are sick" and suggested that they might not be numbered among "the righteous." We don't know whether a single one of them who showed up for Levi's banquet had a clue that they might find a "physician" there—or that they might even require one. But, given the dialogue prompted by the scribes and Pharisees, the members of the "crowd" come face to face with an awareness that someone has perceived them as far from holiness and wholeness.

We are confronted today with that same challenge presented long ago to a motley group of Galilean and Judaean "tax collectors and sinners." If Jesus has sought us out, sat at table with us, and compared himself to the needed physician, it seems that he has done so for reasons a bit more critical than "preventive medicine" or "health maintenance." It seems that he has noticed symptoms of sickness in us.

What are those manifestations that we'd rather deny or ignore? What are those qualities of our persons that are like the bad gall bladder signals after we've eaten fatty foods, like the repeated difficulties we've been having at catching what people say, like the bit of a limp that's developing, like the cough that seems to hang on? And where are those empty corners, jagged edges, searing pains that we somehow know, deep down, we'll never fill, patch, or soothe on our own? Where do we stand most in need of pure, medicinal grace?

11

Jesus, teacher and healer, you see my handicaps and ills, and you know my need for treatment, therapy, cure. Give me an honest knowledge of my need and a deep trust in your care. Help me to remember that you come most readily to those who are broken, those who lack.

FIRST SUNDAY
YEAR A Matthew 4:1–11 • YEAR B Mark 1:12–15
YEAR C Luke 4:1–13

Then Jesus was led up by the Spirit into the wilderness to be tempted by the devil. Matthew 4:1

In Exodus, the desert is the site of the Great Theophany, involving law-giving and covenant-making with the promising but often errant chosen people. In Hosea, the desert is the trysting place where the faithful lover invites the infidel beloved so that he might speak to her heart. In the synoptic gospels—in Matthew, Mark, and Luke—the desert is the setting for Jesus' encounter with wild beasts, satanic temptation, the hunger of fasting, the Father of prayer, and angels.

What might the desert be for us today?

Wherever or whatever it might be, the desert is, by definition, a stark confrontation with the living world at its most elemental. Tumbleweed, scrub juniper, and the saguaro cactus yield no shade from the relentless sun of noonday. Mesa rock, painted sand, and petrified forest warm no bones in night's bitter chill. The wide sky is all stars, but it is cold and faraway and quite bereft of daylight cloud. Most of the rain evaporates before it ever nears the shadowless expanse of flats, arroyos, and canyons. In the desert all we seem to grasp for disappears, like quivering mirage. In such a place there can be an archetypal western "showdown" between the sawed-off soul and God. Meanwhile, we have our horrors of dust devils and coyote howls.

Possession, pleasure, or power may beckon. Or we may be time-tempted: to jump-start the future, to be absent to the present, to hold on to bygones.

However they come, it seems desert moments are a must at some life-turn for anyone who takes the project of being human, humane, and attuned to the divine design seriously. Jesus is presented as survivor and oasis point for the desert-tested. The Word we carry in memory and heart and longing is a living water source.

> When I am driven into dry lands, Lord, feed me with the bread of your word, hold me in a trust that does not test your promises, and warm and cool me in true worship. Help me to remember your love and to face the merciless desert mindful of your mercy.

MONDAY OF THE FIRST WEEK
Matthew 25:31–46

> "Truly I tell you, just as you did not do it to one of the least of these, you did not do it to me."
>
> Matthew 25:45

Those of us who live in cities become rapidly hardened to the plight of the homeless. The first few times we meet one, squat on the street with a ragged cardboard sign in hand with its markered message about a need for food or money, we may well give. We may respond as humanly as we can: get two coffees and donuts for us both to eat, share something from an already packed lunch, ask if we can get the person a hamburger, listen while he or she talks about why the street seems somehow friendlier than the local shelters.

But we soon tire of it. Three or four times on one street we are accosted; one man, whiskeyed red, gets angry when we offer food instead of cash. A woman with a child rejects orange juice. And we retreat into averting our glances, the shrugging apology that we can't reach out and relate to every needy person, the observation that there are hostels and shelters and soup kitchens nearby. Then we decide to shop from now on at a suburban mall where no one lingers at the storefronts with an open violin case and plays for quarters; where no one asks, after we've given to him, if we have something for his buddy down the street. At the mall there are compact discs, Nintendo games, craft shops, sporting goods, lawn furniture sets, camcorders, Reeboks, fabrics, linens, glassware, tool boxes, automotive supplies, housewares, exercise equipment, travel agents, Hallmark cards and gifts, and MAC machines. We spend liberally, because we have been raised to believe that we deserve comfort, relaxation, and toys. When we while away our days in the mall, no one accosts us with a toothless question and an open hand.

The least of our brothers and sisters are safely downtown, on a bench, in a doorway, on a steam grate.

And we are safely where our peace can't be disturbed, where our good will can't be stretched to uselessness by the sheer weight of want. The homeless are protected from our blank stares, and we are shielded from their presence every few yards.

Besides forgetting that the Christ we seek has said he can be found in the very faces we avoid, we also forget that inside these same city limits are people who have seen to it that we have been fed, given drink, clothed, visited, transported, employed, treated in our illnesses—sometimes at *their* expense of time, energy, effort, investment. In an emergency room or a hotel lobby just after we've been robbed, in a traffic accident or in a checkout line when the goods we thought we could carry have gotten too heavy, cordial people have appeared, "angels of mercy." We have been treated, in some moment of need, as if we were the Christ.

This makes it all the more ironic—and unfathomable—that we so easily grow callous to the Christ collapsed on the cement of center city, that we so readily wish him invisible and away.

Soften, O Lord of the bedraggled and bedeviled, my heart that relentlessly turns to stone. Tear down the walls wherein I enclose myself, insuring my safety and guarding my goods against you. I want not to go cold.

TUESDAY OF THE FIRST WEEK
Matthew 6:7–15

"When you are praying, do not heap up empty phrases...." *Matthew 6:7*

No rattling on, Jesus says. And so, every new spiritual movement, every generation, makes up its multiplicity of devotions and long private prayers. It is as if we keep hoping that if we get the words and the gestures right, the pious phrases drummed into our heads and often enough said, they will finally take hold.

No one is saved by hooting out, "Lord, Lord!" Surely we know that. But we keep hoping that we can save something if the drumbeat of "Lord, hear our prayer" or "Holy Mary, Mother of God," or invocations of "Pray for us" directed at St. Jude, St. Anthony, St. Swithin, or St. Margaret of Cortona echo loudly from our vaulted ceilings and rafters.

Prayer, he says, is something more about the heart's desire. It has little to do with repetitions. It is the heart's desire that God-as-a-whole, God above and God below, God beyond and God within, may be revered. It is the heart's desire that God's will and God's design may finally be the harmony of the spheres and that we might sing in tune. That is what we call God's reign, God's kingdom: a cooperative yes to goodness and grace.

Prayer is the heart's desire for bread, for whatever it takes to love. It is the heart's desire for its own forgiveness and for an empathic understanding of others. It is the admission that we have limits of endurance and a resistance that cannot be too hard pressed. So prayer is the heart's wish that we might receive a strong sufficiency, that we might be able to meet life with sufficient strength. It is the hope that hunger, error, sin, hurt, human offense, personal suffering, and world senselessness will never fall upon us altogether too much. Prayer is starting over again and again with the recollection that there is a God, a supremacy, who surpasses all our insufficiencies, knows us, and can somehow carry us along.

The Lord's prayer is a simple request: Great God, be our enough.

There is, after all, very little else much worth saying.

So do. Great God, be my enough too.

WEDNESDAY OF THE FIRST WEEK
Luke 11:29–32

When the crowds were increasing, he began to say, "This generation is an evil generation; it asks for a sign, but no sign will be given to it except the sign of Jonah."   Luke 11:29

Over the eras and eons, humans seem to have raised to the level of fine art the practice of missing the point. We sit inattentively in classrooms and now and then raise our hands to ask for an answer or explanation that has just been given. We buy lottery tickets and put ads in the classifieds suggesting that we are seeking the "SBF" or "SWM" of our dreams and never notice that we already enjoy measures of luck and love that others only long for. We wait for God to do something spectacular for us and never notice that the fact that we are alive *is* monumental and spectacular. We wish restlessly for all to be well even as we are oblivious to the wealth and wellness with which we have already been blessed.

Jesus observed that the people in his own day looked for signs and were eager for esoteric wisdom. Many, too many, missed the point that he himself was not only a sign but the actual incarnation of God. The trouble was that they kept looking around him and far off instead of looking at him. They longed dreamily for an ultimate wisdom to swoop upon them from north, south, east, or west or for a revelation to fall in a lightning flash from heaven and never bothered to listen when the rabbi from unnoteworthy Nazareth spoke on a familiar lakeshore. He was, yes, different but still somehow too commonplace. They had spun legends around Jonah, but this Jesus was just, too many thought, another itinerant preacher. No dazzling stories or mystical sagas, they expected, would be woven around his deeds and warnings. What was so special, after all, about what he said? Repent? Believe? Love? There were some interesting obscurities about the "reign of God" and some fine miracle stories, but the skeptical disdained to be convinced that there was much to him. Yet there were those crowds around him.

How many of their number, how many of those right in front of him, were distracted, disjointed, and missing the point too? Some? Most? All?

We have our crowds of churchgoers as well. And we number ourselves among the "faithful." Can it be that many of us too are given over to the "evil age"—the age of complacency, the age that refuses to see or understand, the age that receives messages but makes no present and personal connections, the age that waits for something else or something down the road a piece? An "evil age" is happily assured that things are going pretty well, that we're basically okay, that no major shakeups are warranted. We've got bits, bytes, microchips of information, so why seek wisdom? And God loves us, loves, us, loves us all. So we'll merrily sing hymns and see life go on blithely and as usual.

Yet all the while we can be missing the point. Jonah, sent by

God, called for radical reform. The Ninevites called a halt and reversed procedures. Jesus, beloved of God, announced good news and called for a change of minds and hearts. Some repented and believed. Paul challenged the early church in Ephesus—those who had already been "converted"—to open themselves to a renewal of their minds. Some thought at least enough of his message to pass it on. The gospel, the living word, reminds us that the call still goes forth: "Reform!" It tells us to reset our sights and look again. It says that we had better do an about-face and measure our paces. Do we?

A prophet may be right before our eyes; the messiah may be once again come; wisdom may be whispering to us at this very moment. And we might be missing the point. Why? Because we think that a revelation of God ought to look or sound like something else. Like something we've never met or heard.

Jesus, however, seems to insist that we keep meeting God, God's wisdom, God's call, God's word. Why, then, do we keep scanning the horizon?

God of wisdom and warning, I look away at just the right or wrong instant. I often find that I want things to remain exactly as they are. And yet I know there is more. I need to be shaken a bit and stopped in my tracks. Push me to look fixedly and help me see the point.

THURSDAY OF THE FIRST WEEK
Matthew 7:7–12

"For everyone who asks receives, and everyone who searches finds, and for everyone who knocks, the door will be opened." Matthew 7:8

Ask, seek, knock. It has become a kind of cliché of spirituality to insist that our asking, seeking, knocking never goes unanswered by God. When we feel we have received no answer to our prayers, the sages tell us, it may be that we are unwilling to accept the answer; the answer perhaps is no, or the answer is long delayed.

Theologians who deal with the great questions of prayer and theodicy have yet to agree on whether or how prayer changes things. Does our prayer postpone a death that God originally planned? Does prayer change not only human history but God's mind?

Then there are those who defer such questions. Prayer, they suggest, is perhaps more a matter of solidarity. Rabbi Harold Kushner urges that prayer is not so much about affecting God's plan as it is about aligning believers in their commitment to well-being and grace and support for one another. Thomas Merton once mused that it was perhaps the prayer of contemplatives and monastics—Christian, Buddhist, whoever—that had so far prevented earthlings from committing nuclear self-obliteration.

In a similar vein, there are those who hold that prayer, at the very least, has to do with a kind of spiritual leverage. In a cosmic tug-of-war, we align ourselves with the forces of good against the forces of evil when we pray.

None of these answer the question of whether human prayer causes God to get up one morning and ease the pain of one burn victim, save the life of a lonely child's grandmother from a car accident, set someone's cancer in remission, change the heart of a spouse bent on divorce, prevent the pursuit of an affair with someone half the prospective pursuer's age, or divert floodwaters away from one old uncle's home. We simply do not know quite enough about the mind of God.

For those of us who persist in prayer—prayer of thanks, praise, contrition, and petition—the fact that we still don't quite know how it "works" can become frustrating. At times, it can discourage us from any prayer at all. Yet, if we examine our personal histories at prayer, we can readily find, as another spiritual cliché has it, that prayer changes *us*, even if it does not change our circumstances or change our God. Perhaps what is and has been most important in our prayer is not the answers but the very asking. When we pray from our deep needs; when we know that we need fish and not snakes, bread and not stones; when we disclose ourselves in a way that admits our lack of self-sufficiency, our weakness, our bare dependency; when we lay our lives out with soulful candor; when we let loose and go defenseless: then surely something can happen.

When we ask and ask and ask, down to the level of our deepest secrets, things change—whether we recognize an answer, a non-answer, a deferral, or a "great maybe" as we wait.

God of far hearing and prayers received, help me to see that prayer does change our human reality. Give me the light to perceive your nearness in my soul-searching, and grant me the honesty that prompts me to admit, "I need." So open me.

FRIDAY OF THE FIRST WEEK
Matthew 5:20–26

"First be reconciled...and then come and offer your gift." Matthew 5:24

What ends in gunfire often begins much earlier in resentment. What ends in suicide often starts as a sentiment that life under certain conditions is intolerable. In either case, the murder or the suicide, someone has become the enemy. Someone has been identified as the source of hurt, as an object of vilification, as an opponent whose very existence is brooded over and regretted. Our enemy can be a very real agent of abuse or injustice. Or the enemy can be manufactured by our prejudiced imaginings. Or the enemy can be the body that fails us and torments when medications and therapies falter.

Jesus of Nazareth was a splendid psychologist. He knew that violence is born of something unreconciled. He urged us to keep going back until we have made some amends or at least come to some peace, bit by bit, even reluctantly. Somewhere along the way we have to settle. If not, the "fool," the offender, the hated, the blameworthy one becomes our target. And we turn into monsters.

God, help me to face and to still the embitterments and angers in my heart. Move me from grudges to peace. Shift my attention from my wounds and losses to life's fine gifts. Give me the glimmers of understanding I need to forgive and to find meaning in pain.

SATURDAY OF THE FIRST WEEK
Matthew 5:43–48

"He makes the sun rise on the evil and on the good, and sends rain on the righteous and the unrighteous."
Matthew 5:45

Not only is freedom of will a principle of the human being's existence, but so too is the freedom of nature to be, to do what it does naturally, apparently a principle of the existence of all creation.

Algae grow, alligators eat, monsoons fall, rivers flood, lions hunt, viruses and bacteria take up residence upon human and non-human hosts, deserts parch, Earth quakes, and spiders catch wispy moths in their delicate webs.

While the Old and New Testaments reveal God's occasional intervention in events, it seems that these are exceptional moments. An Abraham, a Moses, a David, a Jeremiah arises. A Deborah, a Ruth, a Judith, an Esther arrives upon the scene, and history is changed. Manna makes a timely appearance. A non-Jewish king, Cyrus, finds some sense in returning a people to their land and rebuilding their promise. Mary matures in Nazareth and is made ready for whatever extraordinary event God may have in store. Jesus is born. A tomb stands empty because someone who was dead has been raised. Such things do happen, we note. But the ordinary course of things, as the author of Ecclesiastes long ago observed, is that people are born, grow, eat, work, love, become disappointed and disillusioned, weaken, and die. Scoundrels prosper, and good people have their houses cave in. Children sicken, and some starve. Crooks have banquets. And the mediocre go on living their mediocre lives. For the most part, God lets humanity and Earth be, even while God is present wherever wisdom, truth, care, and love reside. The sun shines and the rain falls quite indifferently. That is simply the way, Jesus implies, that things are.

What seems to happen so often is that we find Jesus calling us to accept life and people on their own terms. Beyond that, he calls us to one extraordinary movement: to love all, to love enemies. God perhaps does not change the course of hurricanes or cancer. God does not seem to hold back serial killers or crazed bombers from their passion and paranoia. But God can and does change a whole way of perceiving, a way of being, a way of living at peace in the world.

When enemies are loved, the kingdom of heaven, the reign of God, has come.

But how are we to love our ailments, our natural disasters, our deprivations, our maligners, our attackers? What is lovable in the things and people causing us pain and grief? How are we to see?

God, teach me to look with your love and tolerance. Help me to wait things out patiently. And hold me while your perspective dawns upon me gradually. Guide me to revere what is and to discover the lovable in what, right now, I can hardly bear.

SECOND SUNDAY

YEAR A Matthew 17:1–9 • YEAR B Mark 9:2–10
YEAR C Luke 9:28–36

*And while he was praying, the appearance of his face
changed, and his clothes became dazzling white.*

Luke 9:29

Norman Cousins, in his famed *Anatomy of an Illness,* observed
that arthritic, wheezing Pablo Casals at 90 became another person
once he took up the bow and began to play his cello. He became
the agile, luminous, supple artist consumed in his art. George
Pickering, in his study *Creative Malady,* has told of how chronic illness and phases of invalidism or semi-invalidism were vitally
intertwined with the life projects and productions of Charles
Darwin, Sigmund Freud, Mary Baker Eddy, Florence Nightingale,
Marcel Proust, and Elizabeth Barrett Browning. As they were
engaged in their most brilliant works, the severity of their limits
seemed almost to fall away. And Paul Tournier, in his reflection
Creative Suffering, has noted how many physicians and statesmen
have been orphans. Their vulnerable and difficult backgrounds
did not cripple them but instead equipped them with a drive to
give and to achieve.

What all these studies suggest is that some individuals, certain
figures who have attained notoriety for their creativity and inven-
tiveness, experience transfigurations in their earthly lives. From
and amid their pain, works of beauty, humanity, and ingenuity
are born. And they themselves, the artists and humanitarians and
geniuses, are somehow transformed—made more, made whole—
as they bring their works to fruition.

The transfiguration witnessed by Peter, James, and John on
Mount Tabor revealed that Jesus was more than a mere Galilean car-
penter-turned-rabbi. He was someone who enjoyed a special communion with the whole tradition of the law and the prophets, with

all the great forebears represented by Moses and Elijah. Furthermore, he was in a unique communion with the great "I Am" of Israel, the God for whom he was beloved, the God whom he knew as "Abba." He was more than a man whose legs perhaps cramped as he walked the roadways of Judaea, Samaria, Galilee. He was more than the preacher whose voice perhaps rasped with hoarseness after hours of addressing crowds on the hillsides and shores of Palestine. He was more than one who could bruise, bleed, thirst, and suffocate when they scourged and crucified him.

How the transfiguration of Jesus relates to ours is not altogether clear. He was, after all, divine as well as human by nature. However, we have been promised, by virtue of his resurrection and our baptism, some share in that divinity. And we, simply by virtue of being human, have a capacity for transcendence. Those of us who have tasted self-forgetfulness and strength amid chronic illness have some notion of what that means. A perplexing problem, a project demanding intense concentration, the pressing need of another, the vital conversation—anything that has called forth all the focus and attention of which we are capable—may cause, for a time, a fading away of our pain. A compelling concern can still the havoc wrought by our conditions. We become, for a time, not the usual creaky Casals but pure music. We are not the aching, gasping patient but unadulterated self-gift. We move somehow from being bodies that maintain a fragile sustenance by elaborate medical stratagems to becoming the bone and muscle, nerve and fiber, pulse and breath, mind and heart that are able to revolutionize human thought, reconstruct human well-being, or simply tell the truth of love. How this happens we cannot quite tell.

It must have something to do with the Spirit. Something to do with a mountainous glow.

God of the beyond and the more, Jesus of our hope, raise us. Empower us to beauty, insight, and generous good. Fill us with a strength that transfigures our broken world into something self-surpassing.

MONDAY OF THE SECOND WEEK
Luke 6:36–38

"The measure you give will be the measure you get back." Luke 6:38

Every hospital ward has its favorite patients. Every convalescent home has its well-liked. There are AIDS patients who somehow invite extra attention and devotion. And there are profoundly handicapped people who win popularity contests. How, we wonder, is it? Why do nursing staffs dread dealing with certain patients and welcome others? Why do some sufferers alienate all comers while others seem to cheer their visitors up? Generally the belovedness of certain folks in pain seems to be the direct result of their own attentiveness to and concern for others. Their self-forgetfulness inspires admiration and loyalty. A few examples might illustrate.

While Sister Irene was dying slowly of cancer, part of her daily round was walks up and down the long infirmary hall. The walks were a lengthy business for anyone who walked with her—because she paused at every open door. She looked in on the sisters propped up in bed or held captive in chairs and stopped to chat with them. She listened to the reports of their progress and regress and knew everyone's qualms and problems. She asked after their families and promised prayers. She kept up friendly banter with the aides and nurses and the housekeepers pushing carts of freshly laundered bedding. At night, until she could no longer sit up, she continued to play killer Parcheesi. It was a fast-moving and relentless game laced with laughter. She good-naturedly moved other players' pieces if they dawdled too long after the dice throw. She worried about her aging, never-married sister and got people to write to her and look after her a bit. Sister Irene didn't deny her pain. If asked, she would speak freely of her discomfort. But she refused to dwell on her ailing or her dying.

Hutch had a drawn-out siege of AIDS. He somehow managed to be a "ladies' man" through his hospitalizations. A technologist from the hospital lab brought him vanilla ice cream and volunteered frequently to wash his hair when she noticed it wasn't often being done. Church women came to visit him. The home health nurses enlisted to help when he went home found him endearing. At his next to last public appearance, his 25th high school reunion, he reminisced, told jokes, danced and danced, even though he had to manage with a cane.

No one would ever have charged Hutch with being uncomplaining, because he complained mightily. He had dated a handful of times in the ten-year period since his wife had walked out and left him with their three young children. He must have contracted AIDS on one of those rare dates. He had had some unhappy experiences with medical personnel who didn't want to touch him; and he lost much of the muscle power in his legs when, during one of his extended, fevered hospitalizations, they had declined to get him up and walk him. People who knew him heard all of this. But they also heard his interest in them, for their spouses and kin; and they knew that his thoughts were overridingly on his children. He had raised a vegetable garden, kept house, sewed and cooked for them after his hours of work on power lines. He worried about how his kids were eating and whether the neighbors were really, as promised, keeping an eye on them. Hutch's world was bigger than his AIDS. He spoke of his son's upcoming high school graduation (the one he managed to live to see), the land he wasn't getting planted, how he missed the feel of sun on his back, and how he wanted to be sure that there were no misunderstandings or complications from the jealous husband of the woman who was washing his hair.

Mary Jane and Craig were college students in wheelchairs. Mary Jane was in hers because of a fall from a tree which had broken her back. Craig was born without arms and legs. She tutored people and helped them find their way around the library. She proofread papers and gave pointers when students were studying for tests. She made the dean's list and had an extended plan for learning to drive and for working out residence after graduation. She was headed for one of the helping professions. Craig wrote with a pencil in his mouth; hopped on his stumps from a wheelchair to a desk chair in each classroom, told stories at meals, as he managed somehow to eat neatly without hands or utensils; pledged a fraternity, cheered on the sidelines at athletic events; worked in an office for a political candidate; and served on the orientation committee, greeting a couple of thousand incoming freshmen. Both Mary Jane and Craig knew the facts of their cases and foresaw the extraordinary challenges that doing the most ordinary things would present to them. But they also knew that they had gifts of personality and intelligence. They were not afraid to develop and share these gifts.

The common thread in these all-too-true stories seems to be the other-directedness of the sufferers. Their awareness of issues aside from their own and their commitment to being involved in people's lives saved Sr. Irene, Hutch, Mary Jane, and Craig from some of the potential isolation of their illnesses and disabilities. Their attentiveness to a world beyond their wheelchairs or sickrooms and to the needs of others rendered them likeable. They gave the gifts they had received: gifts of self. From the giving of their gifts, they received in return.

Illnesses, accidents, and birth defects can easily turn us into cranks. We can hold tightly to the little we feel we have left when our "conditions" seem to have robbed us of secure futures, some degree of comfort and freedom, normality. Or we can be grateful for what we have, face our limits squarely, and go on living and giving. The latter seems clearly to be the Christian thing to do. It also seems to be, quite luckily, personally beneficial. "God loves," St. Paul observes, "a cheerful giver" (2 Corinthians 9:7). So, apparently, do a number of human beings—especially when they notice that the giver isn't giving out of his or her own bliss and ease.

Lord, help me to enter into the worlds and worries of others. Guide me to see beyond the clouds and shadows that stand over me and to remember cheer. Then lead me to give it.

TUESDAY OF THE SECOND WEEK
Matthew 23:1–12

"[The scribes and the Pharisees] tie up heavy burdens, hard to bear, and lay them on the shoulders of others; but they themselves are unwilling to lift a finger to move them."   Matthew 23:4

The only ones Jesus is tough on, the only ones who elicit violent language and negative criticism, are the rigorously religious people. Those who strain out gnats and nitpick are the ones who get the sternest castigation. Jesus fumes at them. It's somehow not surprising.

God is altogether simple, says St. Thomas Aquinas. God is love, says St. John. God is an understanding, accepting, forgiving parent, says Jesus—a God who longs only to welcome us home. Why, then, do religious leaders—teachers, preachers, chaplains, pastors, bishops—sometimes fall into the trap of the scribes and Pharisees? Dress codes, pew rentals, tithing checkups, scrupulous cataloguings of mortal and venial sins, prayer lists, certification demands, prerequisites for the reception of sacraments can sometimes press hard the capacities of ordinary folks with ordinary constraints of time, energy, money, and willpower.

We ourselves, even if we have no pulpits, can also—and often do—expect the impossible of people. We can fault them and berate them for failing to be ideal spouses, parents, siblings, children, colleagues, friends, employers, employees, doctors, patients, agents, clients, neighbors. One way or another, we who claim the name of Christian know very well how to communicate to others that they don't quite measure up. It seems they never will.

Perfectionism demanded of ourselves is an affliction; perfectionism demanded of others can be an assault. By contrast, we might recall Jesus' own promise of an easy yoke and a light burden. As we age, we might also find that, as we assess our own inability to conquer certain weaknesses or overcome certain poor habits, we can and should mellow. If we can admit to ourselves that other humans have loved us and that God knows and embraces us with our shortcomings, we ought to be able to concede to others that they need not be stellar, flawless, or canonized to gain our understanding or our smiles.

We can perhaps "lift a finger" to ease and move burdens when we honestly face the fact that we, too, have lifelong burdens that others have eased, shifted, and released by their appreciation for us and acceptance of us as we are. It seems a godly thing to have experienced and a godly thing to do.

Dear God, you love us even as you clearly see us. Help me to be accepting of others, lightening those things that pain and weigh them down. Make sure that I refrain from asking more of others than I myself can offer. Above all, train my eyes to see others with something of your generosity and compassion.

WEDNESDAY OF THE SECOND WEEK
Matthew 20:17–28

Then the mother of the sons of Zebedee came to him with her sons, and kneeling before him, she asked a favor of him. And he said to her, "What do you want?"
Matthew 20:20-21

People inevitably turn to this text in Matthew when they are discussing authority and the concept of "servant leadership." The sons of Zebedee learn that serving others and giving one's life are what being at the right hand and at the left of Christ mean. One of them, James, was dispatched, "killed with the sword," by Herod's order in the early days of the church (Acts 12:2). The other, John, died old. The last word we have of him refers to persecution and exile on the prison island of Patmos (Revelation 1:9). Loyal discipleship, the sons of Zebedee soon discovered, can be very costly.

What is rarely commented on, though, is the short lesson on prayer implicit in the story. The mother of James and John comes to Jesus with all her familial ambitions and misconstruals of his reign. Jesus simply asks her, "What do you want?" When she presents her misdirected request for preferential royal treatment for her sons, she isn't scoffed. She is reminded, though, that there may be a larger picture she isn't seeing. "You do not know what you are asking," Jesus responds (Matthew 20:22). Then the sons and the other ten get some forecasts of how unlike temporal tyranny his reign will really be. They hear that it will be personally demanding in the extreme too.

The two important points we receive, via the mother of Zebedee's sons, are: 1) that the Lord wants us to say, straight out, what it is that we think we want or need; 2) that part of the divine response to our requests can be a call for some reeducation, some perspective shifting on our part. There may be a downside to our petitions. Or there may be something we just "don't get" about our situations—or about God—as yet. The Lord doesn't clobber us for what we don't know or see. He merely asks us to be open to other possibilities.

Meanwhile, we are assured that, no matter how blinkered or silly our concerns may ultimately prove to be, we have One who is waiting to hear them. "What do you want?" is God's question to us daily.

As we mature and enlarge our minds and hearts in grace, we ought to find that the quality of our wants will change.

Lord, let me never fear to tell you what concerns press upon me and what words stir me. But also let me never walk away in haste, chagrined that I don't always get my way. Give me the patience and circumspection to wait and see.

THURSDAY OF THE SECOND WEEK
Luke 16:19–31

There was a rich man who was dressed in purple and fine linen and who feasted sumptuously every day. And at his gate lay a poor man named Lazarus, covered with sores, who longed to satisfy his hunger with what fell from the rich man's table....

Luke 16:19-21

The discomfiting truth is that those of us who buy and read meditation books, attend prayer evenings and renewal days, make retreats amid landscapes studded with western cactus or eastern evergreens, all eat sumptuously by global standards. If we, by an odd set of circumstances, end up for a stretch of months eating raisin bread every morning and peanut butter sandwiches and fruit for each lunch, we tend to think we are suffering extraordinary privation. If the winter heat is poor and we have been sleeping under three blankets and an afghan and still have leg pains because of the cold, we lament the fact that we have had to spend money on an electric heater-fan and have been brewing too much coffee or cocoa or tea just to warm ourselves. When we finally get the chance to move from bone-chilling quarters to a well-heated, shuttered room or suite, and when we finally get to eat somewhere where there's a salad bar, we feel we have recovered a standard of living that is simply normal and human.

The privileged American finds it virtually impossible to grasp that cold quarters and repetitious meals are the most trivial of hardships by worldwide standards. And most of us, even those on low fixed incomes, belong to that category of the privileged. Even if we are at the bottom of the American middle income bracket, we enjoy abundant luxuries. And our luxuries are spiritual as well as material.

Because we are accustomed to lavish comforts and because we measure our impoverishments in terms of monotony, inconvenience, difficulty in managing heat and chill, we find it hard to grasp the pain and deprivation of the Lazaruses at our gates. We find it hard, in fact, to so much as acknowledge that there are people who yearn emptily for a bowl of thin oatmeal or gruel. We find it hard to admit that hordes who sleep in cardboard boxes and makeshift shanties persist. And we find it impossible to disentangle the web of economic systems, political structures, cultural assumptions, and habits of mind and life-style that create, even in this life, an impassible and fixed "great chasm" (Luke 16:26) between ourselves and the lean, longing, vacantly onlooking masses of our brothers and sisters. Often the most we can do is something local—join the Crop Walk, volunteer to ladle out the chili at a shelter, give a bag of groceries to the soup kitchen, pack a box for a Thanksgiving giveaway.

We have not yet learned how to reorder our wants and our world. And we most certainly have not comprehended the challenge that resounded through Yankee Stadium when John Paul II addressed Americans in October 1979:

> The poor of the United States and of the world are your brothers and sisters in Christ. You must never be content to leave them just the crumbs from the feast. You must take of your substance, and not just of your abundance, in order to help them. And you must treat them like guests at your family table.

Why have we instead kept upscaling our "needs"? Why have we not yet come to terms with what our "substance" and our "abundance" might be? Why do we sit cozily, taking our spiritual refreshment, liking our nice, affirming religiosity, and never noticing that, while we are gussied up in "purple and fine linen," people around us are being soothed by the licking of dogs?

God, even today I may well pass someone by as he or she proffers a mug for a handout. Give me the wisdom to know how to respond—when to offer food, when to share a meal, when to drop cash, when to ignore. Like so many, I do not want to buy into an alcohol habit, a drug dose-up. But I don't want to close in on myself either. That is what I find I do. Spare me from blithe feasting while all your poor vanish from my consciousness.

FRIDAY OF THE SECOND WEEK
Matthew 21:33–43, 45–46

"Now when the owner of the vineyard comes, what will he do to those tenants?" Matthew 21:40

35

There is something about us humans that causes us to think of God as a well-organized mastermind who maintains a remote sort of interest in earthly goings-on but has established permanent residence very much elsewhere—in "another country," an incredibly distant one, at that. There is also something about us that tends to reject, assault, even murder those legates who come reminding us of God and of the claims God has on us.

What exactly it is that causes this distancing of God and this disdaining of any reminders of our indebtedness to the Maker of the Universe is quite hard to say. Perhaps it is a bit of greed, our tendency to want to on hold to everything as though it all were ours alone. Perhaps it is a bit of stonewalling, attempting to make God unreachable, forgettable, far away, so that our routines, self-interests, little fiefdoms aren't disrupted or disturbed. Perhaps it is more than a bit of egocentricity. After all, we like to think of ourselves as self-sufficient and beholden to no one.

Whatever the reason for our human resistance to God's sovereignty and self-manifestation, we discover that we can reject God and withhold our giving back only so long. There comes a point at which our inattention and fruitlessness become all too evident—and a point at which we can no longer hold God and human meaning at bay.

Surely, we protest, none of us has killed prophets or the Christ.

We do, however, kill our senses, our sympathies, our spiritual attentiveness, and our impulses to self-surrender and self-giving. We make self-satisfaction and our "stuff" our household gods. We might be observantly "religious," but we'd rather not be bothered by the real, up-close God who tends to expect something of us.

God, I don't really wish to be found slack and wanting. But I realize how easy it is to become "routinized" and superficial. Remind me before it is too late, and remind me again and again that my life is about doing and being for you.

Saturday of the Second Week
Luke 15:1–3, 11–32

So he set off and went to his father. But while he was still far off, his father saw him and was filled with compassion; he ran and put his arms around him and kissed him.   Luke 15:20

The father of the wastrel son is excited and exuberant. At the first sight of the return of the starving scoundrel, he breaks into a run, lavishes the son with affection, and squanders his own goods on a party. Apparently "perfect contrition" wasn't necessary on the part of the son. A bit of hunger and desperation seems to have sufficed. The father is satisfied and exults to see him.

Many of us, schooled in religion, steeped in the "way of perfection," taught to toe the line and persuaded that if we don't possess all virtue we really possess none, have assuredly missed this lesson from Jesus about the bounty of God. If we see the father of the prodigal son as an image of the Father-God, we should be struck by the welcome and festivity he bestows on the son, even though the son only partially "comes to his senses." All we know for sure is that the son finally has figured, in vise-like straits, that he needs his father and cannot go it alone. We don't know whether his confession, with its implied apology, has any depth or whether it is a contrivance to get food.

Whatever mix of motives impels the son homeward—primarily, we suspect, the great gnaw in the gut—he receives a slam-bang homecoming. It is as if to say that God doesn't even care whether we're brought to our knees by sheer want and self-concern or by some monumental insight. God shrugs, having no need of human piety. All that God requires is our recognition that we don't suffice ourselves and that we would be better off in grace.

The parable is very compatible with the 12-step programs' emphasis on our need to acknowledge our own powerlessness over whatever it is that eats us, and also to admit our requirement of guidance and help from a Higher Power. People usually embark on 12-step programs when they bottom out. The prodigal son in Jesus' story certainly had bottomed out and had nowhere to go but home. He didn't necessarily head home with any noble motives or profound resolution. He was simply starved, grubby, and knocked apart.

What he learned was the excessive love of that "higher power" *he* called "Father." What he may have discovered was that, one day at a time, he could remain sober, fed, somewhat in control, and at home. But he first had to learn that his own excesses of dissipation were exceeded only by the excesses of his father's willingness to give and give again and forgive and embrace him.

Lord, I cannot hold my life in check unaided, and I cannot seem to tame the carelessness and will-o'-the-wisp that overtakes me. I turn to you, remembering your provident care and your entirely too much openhandedness.

Third Sunday
YEAR A John 4:5–42 • **YEAR B** John 2:13–25
YEAR C Luke 13:1–9

> The woman said to him, "I know that Messiah is coming." *John 4:25*

The duped, the wrecked, the victims: all of us somehow share their human condition. All of us at some time bear our mistakes or are laid bare in our vulnerabilities.

Like the woman at the well with the five consecutive husbands and the present live-in, we can all too easily fall into things because we're lonely or bereft of affection. Like the sellers and con men in the temple precincts, we can persist in greed or dishonesties because we're tainted and corrupted and too often unthinking. Like the bystanders on whom a tower suddenly collapsed, we can suffer because we have simply been in the way, innocent and taken unawares.

Sometimes we need to be shown that there is another way to love, something finer that is also for us.

Sometimes we need to be caught off guard and have not only our tables but our lives turned over.

Sometimes we need to follow the sixth sense that warns us away, and sometimes we need to stand ready for events in which our mortality catches up with us.

Whatever our case, there is more that we can be, there is something different that we can do. We may not be forcibly and dramatically turned around. That is to say, we may not outright have an encounter with God in the town square or at a watering place. We may not have our life work upset and our projects shown to be shabby. And we may not be rescued from cave-ins, accidents, or the crash of things around us. But we can, in all cases, stand integral and ready.

We can opt to pursue love and wealth honorably and well. We

can recall that our lives are contingent. We can, at our very core, surrender our lives to God and live peaceably with our want and our need. We can know, as St. Augustine discloses in his *Confessions,* that we are unfulfilled and misdirected when left to our own devices, that our hearts will always be restless until we rest in God.

We can, if we attend to the voice of wisdom, come to know God "in spirit and truth" (John 4:23). We can enter into the "Father's house" and be consumed with zeal (John 2:16–17). We can repent and bear fruit and face our perishing with equanimity because we are confident that our souls will not be lost (Luke 13:3, 5).

I need, O God, and I want. I try to fill my blankness and void with cheap loves and clutter and sometimes I go carelessly. Call me back to finer things, to the bliss of being, to you as my destiny.

MONDAY OF THE THIRD WEEK
Luke 4:24–30

And he said, "Truly I tell you, no prophet is accept-ed in the prophet's hometown." Luke 4:24

Sometimes the truth of something or someone can be rejected because it seems too ordinary. Herbal cures, swims in warm streams, the addition of certain fruits or vegetables to one's daily fare, vigorous walking all seem far too uncomplicated as routes to health and healing. We more readily accept exotic regimens of pill-taking and injections, exercise routines on expensive cycles and NordicTracks, high-tech appliances and electro-massage equipment than simple suggestions about diet and movement in open air. Similarly, members of our families, parishes, communities can repeatedly go unheard when they make observations or recommendations that challenge what is customary and comfortable to us. We'd far prefer to bring in pricey facilitators and consultants and counselors. For some reason, we seem to give these latter far more credence than folks we know. We pay for "expertise" often when some very local perceptions and common sense could do as well.

Jesus' counsel and his person seemed far too down-to-earth, too plain, too humble in language and origins for his townspeople to take. They would rather that he'd come from afar, a wild stranger, performing arcane rituals and enunciating exotic, indecipherable admonitions. He likely would then have been deemed more wise, holy, and possessed of expertise. Instead, he came among them as a poor boy, a carpenter, a speaker of Aramaic with homespun parables and simple, direct words about God, the good, and human love. He unrolled familiar scrolls and applied them to the world and the people they already knew. What good in that?

We, too, await signs and marvels and the Second Coming of Christ. We are poised in readiness for prescriptions that require us to do somersaults and fly to mystic spas and undertake unthinkable missions. Meanwhile, we shun opportunities to cross the street, talk honestly with someone, and meet the stranger's eye. We decline to divest our lives of complexity and contradiction. That would seem too facile, too uninteresting, too blasé.

What we have yet to learn is how powerfully God and God's truth can be present in the everyday.

Lord of truth and obviousness, break through my fixations on the novel, the fabulous, the abstruse. Show me your presence in the immediate and the near. Give me eyes to see and ears to hear the wonder around me.

TUESDAY OF THE THIRD WEEK
Matthew 18:21–35

"And in anger his lord handed him over to be tortured until he would pay his entire debt. So my
heavenly Father will also do to every one of you, if
you do not forgive your brother or sister from your
heart."   *Matthew 18:34-35*

One of the most inexplicable of our traits is the difficulty we have
in extending to others the consideration that has been shown to
us and we have come to expect. The elderly grow impatient with
other elderly as they move slowly or mis-hear. The member of a
minority group who has had to fight for her rights becomes intol-
erant of the new minorities as they speak new words, new patterns, and seem to jibber-jabber. The woman who has had to clear
hurdles of sexism to attain a professional position is relentlessly
tough on the woman coming up in her field. The parent or teacher
who had a lonely, pained adolescence forgets to listen for the
undertones in a teen's demands, complaints, questions; the adult
instead criticizes the bagginess of pants, the mismatch of layers of
shirts, the angle of a cap, the cut of hair. We all somehow forget
that, no matter how rugged our struggle, some one or two along
the way did the favor, said the encouraging word, rekindled our
fire, or just watched on the sidelines patiently and quietly cheered.

When we fail to extend to others the helping hand, when we
fail to give the boost, when we decline to see that someone is
where we have been and needs what we have needed, we have to
suspect ourselves of both ingratitude and bitterness. Ingratitude
forgets that someone, somewhere along the way, has gone the
extra mile for us. Bitterness remembers the struggle and hurt and
still resents it. Both ingratitude and bitterness turn us inward on
ourselves. And so we see where we need comfort, how we
deserve rest, why we shouldn't be expected to lift a finger, what

we need to protect our turf; and all the while the one who wants our understanding and warmth meets incomprehension and chill. The one who looks to us for mercy meets mercilessness.

Among the messages of this parable of the unforgiving servant is a warning that our lack of compassion, our grudge-holding, our unforgivingness will come back to torment us. It may not only be a tortured afterlife we face. It may also be a here-and-now in which we are bereft of company, avoided by colleagues, left to the devices of our own stinginess, straitjacketed in the unfeeling of our hard hearts. What then?

> Lord, help me always to recall that I have been forgiven, assisted, encouraged, understood at moments of my most dire need. Don't let me turn away, disdaining others' pain and lack. Make me free to give from what I have received—and even generous enough to give as I wish had been given to me.

WEDNESDAY OF THE THIRD WEEK
Matthew 5:17–19

> "Do not think that I have come to abolish the law or the prophets; I have come not to abolish but to fulfill."
>
> Matthew 5:17

What law? What prophets? That is part of the problem with which this text leaves us. But it isn't the hardest problem. We have, after all, Jesus' own sense that the law is fulfilled by love—wholeheart-ed, single-minded love of God and compassionate, self-giving love of neighbor. So, too, are the prophets fulfilled: by an uncon-ditional return to God, by the eviction of our idolatries, by a new attentiveness to the cry of the poor. Micah (6:8) has summed it up for us: it is our charge "to do justice, and to love kindness, and to walk humbly with your God." Whatever expresses, promotes, defends, manifests, celebrates genuine love fulfills the law and the prophets. Whatever shies away from, shuns, compromises, or denies love undoes the law and the prophets just as surely as acts of violence, hatred, oppression, abuse, and manipulation do.

The real problem, though, is not a matter of simple comprehension of Jesus' meaning. We can put it together fairly well at six o'clock in the morning, over lunch, or just before we go to sleep. If we know Jesus at all, we know that his call is love. The problem is that we all tend to "abolish the law and the prophets," indeed to abolish love, as soon as we meet conflict, disappointment, or someone who is disagreeable to us. As soon as we start fixating on what others should be doing but aren't, how they should treat us but don't, why they should be otherwise and yet refuse to change; when they should consider us and our rights but instead run over us roughshod, how everything would be so much better if it ran *our* way—then we have begun undoing the law and the prophets.

Fulfilling the law and the prophets seems to be a matter of self-emptying, a matter of trying as best we can to see the broader vista, a bit as God sees it, a matter of walking in others' shoes, standing for some moments within their experience.

If we are honest, we recognize that we never quite do that. We may discover that where we most need conversion to the love that Jesus tells us he "fulfills," is in the most ordinary places: in our traffic behavior, in our post office and grocery line attitudes, in our telephone conversations, in our dealings with our on-the-job irritants, in our living rooms or bedrooms at night when we have taken off our shoes.

Lord, teach me to commit love rather than sin. Correct my seeing and open me to empathy so that I might understand rather than judge and condemn, so that I might open my arms rather than close my fists.

THURSDAY OF THE THIRD WEEK
Luke 11:14–23

Others, to test him, kept demanding from him a sign from heaven.   Luke 11:16

When a man who has been mute can suddenly speak, some people are sure that it is some dark magic, some satanic influence, a diabolical power that has dazzled them. Others think it might be an act of God, a manifestation of good, but they want a guarantee, a double-check, a direct and unambiguous "sign from heaven" as reassurance. We moderns are not so prone to ascribe astonishing events to demonic forces as the ancients were, but we are similarly reluctant to credit God for our good fortune, happy surprise, reversal of what seemed a dreary fate. We are more likely to attribute the unexpected—especially if it is vastly improbable—to luck, chance, accident, coincidence. We are very wary of seeing the "finger of God" as the one tracing the lines of our healings, successes, loves, triumphs, benefits. It is easier just to shrug and say that we don't know why or how such wonderful things have befallen us.

Maybe it has something to do with our scientific worldview. We believe in randomness, uncertainty, chaos. Charles Darwin, Werner Heisenberg, and James Gleick have told us about these. Science has challenged our fixities and simplifications—and rightly so. It has made us cautious of platitudes about "God's will" and mistrustful of hastily naming certain turns of events "miracles." That also seems right. We need humility more than we need certainties, and we need an appreciation of multiple causation and complexity more than we need confident, glib explanations. We might chide theoretical physicists in their search for a "G.U.T." or a "T.O.E."—a "grand unified theory" or a "theory of everything"—as if discovering such would explain the whole cosmos.

But we also should be chided if we want to make everything mystical and supernatural and thus overlook the ordinary and the natural. Still, we should be chided even more severely if we want to take things that transcend nature and write them off as delusions, deceptions. Jesus reminds his hearers that good results have Goodness itself at their root. The action of God in nature and beyond nature is not self-contradictory or self-combatting. The natural does not diminish the supernatural, and an explanation does not detract from the godliness of some good that has seemed inexplicable.

Every now and then a mute person speaks. A cancer disappears. A patient with AIDS outlasts all lifespan predictions. A scientist with ALS (Stephen Hawking) researches, teaches, and writes best-sellers from a wheelchair. Jesus urges that evil doesn't author such things. By whatever means available—prayer, optimism, medical technology, nature's self-correction—God accomplishes them. Good things themselves are God's "sign."

Lord, let me trust the Good I experience and see, grateful for your handiwork.

FRIDAY OF THE THIRD WEEK
Mark 12:28–34

When Jesus saw that he answered wisely, he said to him, "You are not far from the kingdom of God."
Mark 12:34

Sometimes the essence of wisdom is recognizing the truth of someone else's interpretation and teaching. Sometimes it is being able to get to the heart of the matter. When the scribe hears Jesus' delivery of the two great commandments, he recognizes them immediately as a fine summary of the law. A good listener, he is able to feed back to Jesus what he has just said, and he also adds his own note: that wholehearted love of God and fulsome love of neighbor "is much more important than all whole burnt offerings and sacrifices" (Mark 12:33). This scribe not only knows the core of the law; he also understands how it orders priorities.

Answering wisely is no easy matter. For the scribe to be able to do so, he must have spent many pensive hours—solitary moments leaning against a large rock, gazing out across desert; cool moments under the shade of a tree watching the buzz of townspeople; slow moments as the moon traversed the night sky, reviewing his days, his pathways, and asking what they all might mean. Being wise and behaving wisely are even more difficult. One can answer wisely and yet not act wisely at all.

We all know armchair philosophers and porch-sitting sages. They have reality in general, human motivation, personal priorities, the tangle of right and wrong, good and evil, and the broad lines of God's design pretty well figured out. But they rarely move from their armchairs and porches. And so we wonder what their wisdom serves. Who benefits? Only those who happen by? Does it suffice to sit still and come to some clarity, as a Zen Buddhist?

We have to ask ourselves if we are the armchair philosophers, the front porch sages, the astute scribes. Do we have correct order, sure truths, keen insights ready at hand? But do we still have to face that, while we are "not far from" the realm of God, we have not arrived? Do we know the map but delay taking the trip?

Wise teacher, show me not only what to know but where and how to go. Set me journeying in love.

SATURDAY OF THE THIRD WEEK
Luke 18:9–14

But the tax collector, standing far off, would not even look up to heaven....   Luke 18:13

The tax collector is the picture of dejection, of a life that has caved in. He is the mid-lifer in turmoil, the settled one who has become unsettled in wondering how to cope *"When All You've Ever Wanted Isn't Enough"* (to use Harold Kushner's title). Or he is the moderately good person who is now browbeating himself for the awful mistake he has made or for the startling sin he hadn't known he was capable of committing. Whatever the reason, the tax collector is downcast. And he is at the point of realizing that he can't pick himself up, pull himself together, set things right, get on with life. He has nowhere to go but into a flat-out appeal for God's mercy.

He is at the AA moment of recognizing his powerlessness. There is no resource to fall back on except a Higher Power not his own.

We have these moments. Some of us have many of them. Any review of our accomplishments or any recitation of our good deeds, virtues, and gifts becomes absurd, meaningless. We know that we are fragile flesh and irresolute spirit and that we go on only by God's grace.

When we do cast ourselves empty-hearted and empty-handed into God's care, we do find, however, that we can eventually look up again. We notice that there is twilight, dark night with clouds sweeping away the moon, but then the swaths of lavender, pink, blue-gray, yellow that signal sunrise. We discover that the world still turns. And somehow we can go home. And begin again. "Justified," it says (Luke 18:14).

Jesus, merciful, remake my heart. And as you do so, reconstruct my life from the shambles I have dully made. Send confidence. Send saving grace.

FOURTH SUNDAY
YEAR A John 9:1–41 • YEAR B John 3:14–21
YEAR C Luke 15:1–3, 11–32

"And this is the judgment, that the light has come into the world, and people loved darkness rather than light because their deeds were evil." John 3:19

It seems that there can hardly be any place darker than a thickly wooded campsite on a moonless night when the fire has died and the flashlight suddenly burns out. Darker still, though, is a deep cave when lanterns extinguish and all that there is of life and direction seems to be the flap of bats.

Those of us who are sighted can only recall such moments when we try to imagine what it might be not to see at all. Yet all of us are somehow linked to the experience of the speaker of one of Robert Frost's poems: "I am one acquainted with the night." If we have not known the density of impenetrable physical dark, if we have not had nights when our sense of place was lost and we stood helpless and in dread, we have perhaps not known in our senses and skin the darkness of the man born blind. But we have perhaps known black confusion. We have perhaps, like the prodigal son, wallowed in some darkness we have chosen. We have also, it may be, stood in the grim shadow of depression or felt the darkness of our sin closing in. Some smothering midnight has sometime touched us; some curtain has wrapped around us like a tourniquet.

At times, it may even have been that we were so steeped in darkness, so trapped in mire, so lost and senseless of north or east or down or up that we began to believe we could love the dark. We held it tight and close.

But something in the pit of the stomach signaled that we could gain, in the dark, no sureness of foot. We could not go, and we could not know *where* to go.

When Jesus speaks of light, he speaks of panorama, of depth perception, of color, of clarity.

He stands, in himself and in the wholeness of his life, for the opening of eyes and a road home.

Goodness is signal flare, warm fire, hearth light. It is beacon, lantern, moon sliver, swarm of fireflies.

Daybreak is the love we choose that wakes us from what would be loveless, endless night.

Lord, when blackout covers me, or when I'm face-down and dead-eyed in sin, recall the light. Come as moon, star, sun.

MONDAY OF THE FOURTH WEEK
John 4:43–54

Jesus said to him, "Go; your son will live." The man believed the word that Jesus spoke to him and started on his way. John 4:50

"Visualizing" has been something of a rage, in neap and flood tide fashion, for a number of years now. Golfers are taught to visualize the hole-in-one, football players to visualize the winning kick. Students are taught to visualize success in projects and tests. Cancer patients are taught to visualize little armed warriors blitzing away their cancer with laser guns and star-wars technology. People in therapy are taught to visualize themselves as children again, being held and comforted as they wish they had been. There seems to be something to it, this picturing of the completed goal, the healed wound.

Years ago Norman Vincent Peale sold Americans on "The

Power of Positive Thinking." Creative visualization and positive thinking are indeed routes to victory, achievement, health, emotional well-being, and reconciled relations with others. What happens in this story of Jesus and the official and the sick boy in Capernaum, however, goes beyond visualization and positive thought. The depths of faith well up as the man goes with assurance, and yet with no physical evidence, that his boy will be vigorous and whole again.

The creative visualizer and the positive thinker do concentrated work. The person of faith who appeals to the Lord on behalf of his son does no work whatsoever—except the work of request and surrender. The official lets go, knowing there is nothing he or any earthly power can do. He takes Jesus at his word and departs with confidence. He doesn't have to cultivate a particular mental state or exert his imagination. There is something wordless and effortless in him as he turns to head home. When his faith is confirmed by the good news of the boy's recovery, it passes to an even deeper level, a level of conviction and commitment that will extend beyond a single illness or an isolated episode.

For us, creative visualization and positive thinking are very empowering—and therefore are salutary, beneficial. Faith is somehow both disempowering and empowering. It catches us in collapse, supports us in weakness, lets us be still in our need. Yet faith also strengthens, resolves, affirms, assures. The difference is that the power we rely on in faith is not our own—and mercifully doesn't have to be.

Lord, thank you for the faith that saves lives and saves me. I need. Remind me that I need not rely on my own strength and resources for the life and good that can be. I come empty-handed and waiting.

TUESDAY OF THE FOURTH WEEK
John 5:1–3, 5–16

At once the man was made well, and he took up his mat and began to walk. Now that day was a sabbath.

John 5:9

The Hebrew word *shabbat* means rest, repose, completion, a cessation of activity. Both human wisdom and divine revelation indicated to the people of ancient Israel that a day was needed regularly—and frequently—for putting aside chores, humdrum tasks, and menial work. A day was needed for refocusing and for the consideration of ultimate things and ultimate Being. To take a sabbath was understood to be a holy and wholesome thing.

The conflict that arises when Jesus does a good work on the sabbath—when he reaches out to heal a sick, weak man and set him walking, carrying his mat—is the kind of thing that happens when a fine custom and a godly command get mystified. Forgetting that *shabbat* has to do with restoration and the reordering of priorities, the "holy ones" bristle when Jesus *does* something. As far as they are concerned, it matters little that a good deed has been done. They are preoccupied with its not being the right way, the right time; Jesus has not acted in strict compliance with rubrics. He has done a good thing on the wrong day.

We, too, can be petty and can persecute those who violate convention. We can forget that there are occasions that call for a bending of rules. When people are free and whole, God's sabbath is present. When people are entangled in red tape and constrained by propriety, the wearying, workaday week holds reign. We forget how to make a humane response and how to unlink chains. And we get no sabbath ourselves because we take no rest from the business of watching whether everyone else is doing the "right" thing the "right" way on the "right" schedule. We leave no room for pure goodness and grace.

God, grant that I may carry a sabbath in my heart and
that I may follow, in you, the law of freedom.

WEDNESDAY OF THE FOURTH WEEK
John 5:17–30

"The hour is coming when all who are in their graves
will hear [the Son of Man's] voice and will come
out—those who have done good, to the resurrection of
life, and those who have done evil, to the resurrection of condemnation."   John 5:28-29

What you are in your youth, you'll be in old age—except in exag-
gerated form. Such a sentiment is frequently expressed among
administrators of homes for the aged, nurses, and especially people who have watched for a good portion of their lives the aging
processes of those around them. Apart from those whose personalities undergo change or deterioration because of medication,
strokes, dementia, or Alzheimer's, the general rule for seniors
seems to be that their personalities do not so much alter; rather,
they become quite set. The demanding, persnickety 90-year-old
was a crank in his 40s. The genteel, patient lady in the wheelchair
was cordial and welcoming at 35. The downbeat had the art of
pessimism refined even as young marrieds. The upbeat had a *joie
de vivre* in high school. The compliant, easygoing, unexcitable
types learned early how to shrug and go on. People who knew
them can tell you these things at their golden anniversaries, eight-
ieth birthdays, diamond jubilees.

What Jesus seems to say here runs in the same vein. Our lives,
in spite of rare disruptions and inconsistencies, follow patterns. We
establish for ourselves certain modes of behavior, certain trends of

response, certain habits of mind and action. If we have learned kindness, concern, and acceptance of life on its own terms, we can generally count on lifelong manifestations of these selfsame ways of being. If we have cultivated grudges, self-centeredness, and irritability, we will reap the same. These patterns of behavior and characteristics of our being we carry with us as the years tick by, hour after hour. We carry them too, says Jesus, into eternity.

Those who have loved well and acted with genuine *caritas* rise to heaven because they have already entered into something of what it is to be heavenly. They have become acquainted with the lovingness of God and have embraced God's word. Those who have faced life, the world, and their sisters and brothers with contempt go down to misery. They have rejected mercy, forgiveness, the nudgings and whisperings of God. Misery is, as a result, all they can finally know.

In the niches of our personalities, we can grow godly. And godliness will flow like an ever-renewing stream. In the crags and corners of our consciences we can also grow hellish. And hell will boil over as from a cauldron wherever we go.

We *do* "take it with us." In this life and into the next, we take ourselves...particularly the selves we have made.

God of life, where there are seeds of a generous will, let them spring up and flourish. Send drought to what is damnable. Let me nourish and tend the better self you wish me to grow to be.

THURSDAY OF THE FOURTH WEEK
John 5:31–47

"He was a burning and shining lamp, and you were willing to rejoice for a while in his light."   John 5:35

The fickleness of fame, adulation, and popularity is no new thing. It is not just a late-twentieth-century phenomenon that the rising star of the top forty fades from remembrance, that the acclaimed performer or politico falls into oblivion.

In Jesus' day, hosannas gave way to demands for crucifixion in barely a week. John the Baptizer had disciples, and yet when he was beheaded some forgot to lament.

For generations, it seems, we humans have had the sorry habit of transferring our loyalties from one person to the next as winds blow, as new fads arise, as the weather shifts, as our moods and hormone levels alter. There is not much testimony to fidelity. Today's hero may be tomorrow's scapegoat or villain; today's celebrity, tomorrow's castaway.

When heroes or celebrities challenge us, sting our consciences, stir our souls, their hold on us may be the most fleeting of all. We tire when awakened; we wear thin when we feel too stretched. We prefer to go back to quiet, comfortable living rooms and an occasional outburst of televised laughter when we are too shaken or piqued. Our ability to sustain confrontation or to follow through on the twists and turns that conversion calls for are short-lived.

Mohandas Gandhi attested to the great attractiveness of the person of Jesus of Nazareth, the power of his message, the strident urgency of his ways. He also remarked that he had yet to see Christians who lived their faith with any notable consistency.

Today's Christians, most of us, may be disciples only nominally. We have perhaps been better schooled in polls, fads, trend-setting, and shattering, kaleidoscopic change than in the steadfastness of the gospel. We flash dance and spotlight, skip out and show up on the next block.

Jesus says that John the Baptizer burned and shone. He lit an Olympic flame that led to Jesus and thus to light and life. We, though, prefer a flicker. We refuse to stand in a single, strong light too long.

Lord, though I have let you be light for a while, I have backed into shadow and then run to lesser lights. Shine on me again, and help me to live in your brightness and clarity, on and on. Amen.

FRIDAY OF THE FOURTH WEEK
John 7:1–2, 10, 25–30

Now some of the people of Jerusalem were saying, "Is not this the man they are trying to kill? And here he is, speaking openly, but they say nothing to him! Can it be that the authorities really know that this is the Messiah? Yet we know where this man is from; but when the Messiah comes, no one will know where he is from."   John 7:25-27

We like our teachers and prophets, our doctors and presidents properly certified, reputable, and well-born. There may be a certain charm about stories of leaders born in log cabins who struggled for literacy and learning and managed to become stunning orators; there may be a certain attraction to narratives of youths stricken with multiple handicaps who become theoretical physicists and write best-selling books; but generally we prefer the ladder to success to have straightforward, predictable steps.

We look askance if the surgeon did his premed at Slippery Rock College. We raise a quizzical eyebrow if the author is rumored to be dyslexic. We wonder why the Ph.D. in front of us is none too astute at Aristotle or renders French phrases with a barbaric accent. We would rather our friends and our betrothed be from the posher residential areas and not have a cousin in jail.

Messiahs, even two millennia ago, were not supposed to come

from unknown villages or crossroad towns. They weren't supposed to engage in ordinary crafts and trades. They weren't expected to be of dubious parentage. Better, it was thought, that they be regal, erudite, steeped in mystery, pedigreed.

Jesus, though, had this disreputable air about him. They watched him, monitored his comments, then played it—the authorities, that is—nonchalant. They distanced themselves and left the unruly crowd to question why they didn't disturb him, this once, in Jerusalem. Better, perhaps, just to leave the impression that Jesus was, as far as they were concerned, inconsequential. The hangers-on, meanwhile, scratched their heads and asked messianic questions as they tried to ascertain who, after all, this Nazarene might be.

He didn't fit their expectations. The power of his words didn't mesh with the persona. Dusty feet, calloused hands, and the Galilean dialect all seemed to discredit him.

We of the nearly-twenty-first century watch and wait too. We have been told that the Savior will come again. And he himself proclaimed that we could meet him in the "least." It is, however, inconceivable to us that Holy Wisdom might break forth in the naggings of a rumpled crone or the jive of a drummed-up rapper. It's unseemly to recall the Lord of Life in the amputee propped on his crutch who begs by the drugstore window. We can't quite picture the Anointed One with AIDS or under late-night gunfire. We don't expect a gospel from a battered face or an untended cry.

Like the dissemblers and the seekers in old Jerusalem, we would rather our God be tidied up, high-class, refined, elegant, unanimously esteemed, and cordial. We could handle manifestations of the Messiah so much more readily if they would just trouble themselves to be respectable. And we could respond so much more genteelly if we were sure that God would station himself or herself quite far above us.

I am troubled, God, to think of you as scruffy and rough-neck. You are altogether too much for us, and yet you persist in appearing as less than, and so different from, what we prefer and expect. Open my eyes, Lord. Reeducate my religious imagination.

SATURDAY OF THE FOURTH WEEK
John 7:40–53

But some asked, "Surely the Messiah does not come from Galilee, does he?"   John 7:41

It is, at least, a question. Jesus caused "division in the crowd," it says (John 7:43). The chief priests here, the gullible crowd there. The Pharisees here, discreet Nicodemus and some indiscreet fishermen elsewhere. There were skeptics, and there were the entranced.

One of the great fallacies logicians point to is *argumentum ad hominem:* the discrediting of an idea that is based on a discrediting of the one who presents it. Character assassinations and political smears are used against a proposal. Innuendoes about the proposer are advanced against the theory. Logicians recognize the tactic and its fatal flaw, but it continues to be used because it is so frequently effective.

It is a sickness of our society and our political processes, this ultimate dirty pool. Defamation and detraction tilt our elections and keep tabloids in business. Scandals sully our educational establishments and our charities and our pulpits. Eventually we find ourselves mistrusting every noble sentiment and suspecting a scheme underneath each act of altruism.

Jesus suffered prejudice, bad-mouthing, slander, and putdowns. Perjury and chicanery led to crucifixion. At least some of it started with today's story: the conviction that no one from his class, no renegade Galilean, could be worth anything. No lofty inspirations, no piercing prophecies could possibly come from his dunghill section of the country. At the crisscross of culture and trade routes, those from Galilee were ruffians and degenerates. Nothing but a travesty of Judaism, nothing but spiritual corruption and inanities, could come from them.

Classism and libel worked some of their malice against him. The wonder is that some few managed, amidst it all, to think for themselves and listen.

They knew that there had to be more to Jesus than the story of his origins. There had to be more, too, to God's machinations than the limits of territory and presuppositions.

The faithful who didn't dismiss him were blessed with the capacity to see through bias. They were free enough to trust their intuitions and make considered judgments of what was true and good on its own merits. They left their souls unfettered and opened their hearts to one who spoke their language and seemed to know their unsung songs. In the end, they didn't care what he seemed to be or where he was said to be from. There was more to him than a set of unsavory stories.

They continued to speak of him.

It is a wonder that we do.

Preserve me from suspiciousness of soul and narrowness of mind. Spare me from making condemnations that are the downfall of great ideas and splendid persons. Help me, Lord, to suspend judgment until I have seen and heard, and deflect me from the prejudgings of ill will and biases. I seek you, Lord, and truth.

FIFTH SUNDAY

YEAR A John 11:1–45 • YEAR B John 12:20–33
YEAR C John 8:1–11

So the sisters sent a message to Jesus, "Lord, he whom you love is ill." But when Jesus heard it he said, "This illness does not lead to death; rather it is for God's glory, so that the Son of God may be glorified through it." John 11:3-4

In his classic *Varieties of Religious Experience,* William James develops a profile of those most likely to be susceptible to dramatic, life-altering religious conversions and those less likely to experience a major upheaval. The susceptible, convertible types he calls "sick souls." Those likely to be amiably content with life and belief, as is, he calls "healthy-minded." The latter are optimistic, quite well-integrated, inclined to a rather blithe pantheism, James believes. People like Walt Whitman who "hear America singing" don't go looking for conversion experiences—and are not likely to be found by them either, James proposes.

The ones who *are* likely to be receptive to and rerouted by a transforming spiritual experience are people like St. Augustine, Martin Luther, and a host of other startling "converts." These are people who are "divided selves," aware of a certain all-askew quality in themselves and often overwhelmed by the ambiguities and evils of the world. They are in touch with their personal inadequacies and with life's inconsistencies. They may also be, James suggests, more responsive to what is going on, on their own subliminal levels, and more ready to attend to their intuitions. A kind of divine discontent, a yearning for wholeness, and a sense of the sacred open them to the touch of God.

While we can question how "healthy-minded" a kind of cheerful, pollyannish complacency can really be, we have to admit that James seems to be on to something about the "convertible" personality.

God can reach us in our depths only if we have opened up and let ourselves be reachable. We can stand in God's light only if we have somehow exposed ourselves. We can hear only if we are listening for something. And we will accept the ministrations of the Divine Physician only if we recognize in the first place that there is something in us in need of healing.

A man who has had a death experience and a memory of an entombed awakening like Lazarus' would certainly know that his life needed some repair, some restoration. So, too, would his two sisters, who saw their security torn away, their faith teased and then confirmed, and then had to live a life in amazement at the doings of one they had called "Lord," only half-conscious of the implications. So, too, would a woman who stood in disarray, publicly accused and publicly ashamed, rescued and mystified by a stranger, and aware forever after that she had been a near-miss for a stoning to death. All of these people could be, in one way or another, described as "sick souls" who were touched by Jesus and led to glory. The gospels memorialize them.

Jesus teaches that the grain of wheat must "die" if it is not to remain a stunted, ungerminated, ungrowing grain (John 12:24).

Everyone who has been converted to Jesus, everyone who has been "born again" or who has undergone some grand return, has certainly experienced some sickness, some death. Some aspect of self, some facet of life, has led to that gnawing for more and that covering over that welcomes rain and then warmth and then sun and the light of day.

And everyone who has truly turned to Christ in her heart, in his, has experienced growth and burgeoning.

William James says that genuine conversions are rarely reversible. The ailing who have come to health, the "sick souls" that have been made well, will not exchange a present, blessed state for a former, beleaguered and plagued one. Those who would go back, or those who do, simply show that they have not been sane. They have not sprung up, nor have they been raised at all.

The question is what state of growth or health we find our-selves in. Or are we still encased in seed shell or tomb?

Lord of growing up and altering, alter me. Call me forth and water me. If I am sick, as I have been, lay your hands on me and lift.

MONDAY OF THE FIFTH WEEK
John 8:1–11

The scribes and the Pharisees brought a woman who had been caught in adultery; and making her stand before all of them, they said to him, "Teacher, this woman was caught in the very act of committing adultery. Now in the law Moses commanded us to stone such women. Now what do you say?"

John 8:3-5

One rendering of what Jesus is doing in this encounter with the adulteress when he twice stoops to write on the ground is expressing boredom with the proceedings. If nothing of interest is going on, if one wishes to disconnect and get on with one's own thoughts and imaginings, the ideal way is to doodle—even to doodle in the dust.

Jesus would rather not get entangled in a self-righteous blame game, and he does not care to dignify the question of stoning as punishment with a dead-on side-taking.

Instead, he deflects the attempt to trip him up on a matter of law and observance, and he decenters those who pride them-selves on catching someone else in a forbidden act.

The response that sends the elders slinking away—"Let anyone among you who is without sin be the first to throw a stone at her" (v. 7)—trounces the accusers. But so too does the casualness of Jesus' demeanor—the stooping, the playing of his index finger in the dust, the straightening, the short comment, the stooping again, the further doodling.

And in the end he has little to say. The woman hears no castigation about passion, sin, sex; no admonition to self-control or repentance. She simply meets assurance that she is not condemned—and the inference that she is understood. The advice to stay clear of the self-compromise and sin is delivered to her gently.

Jesus demonstrates that he finds self-appointed judges tedious, ploys to trap him in a double-bind dismissable, and the use of a woman as a public pawn dehumanizing. He scribbles in the sand and bides his time even as he forces the hands that would hurl rocks to ungrip and, sooner or later, drop them.

We North Americans tend to take a prurient interest in the sexual misdeeds of others. We inhabit a land where XXX movies, adult book stores, sleazy talk shows, and the pornography industry flourish even while pledges to restore the death penalty and to ease gun laws tend to cinch elections. We ought perhaps to watch more closely the Lord who finds our erotic fascinations dull and our bloodlust too stupid to merit comment. He leaves us dumbfounded: with our secrets locked in the recesses of memory and stones stilled in our hands.

Lord, before I judge and begrudge, quiet me. Recall to me your calm and your love. Keep me far from destructive tactics and the machinations that make our streets a frenzy. Let me look in the eyes of those "caught in the act," whatever it may be, and see there a sister, a brother, your friend.

TUESDAY OF THE FIFTH WEEK
John 8:21–30

"And the one who sent me is with me; he has not left me alone, for I always do what is pleasing to him."

John 8:29

The "Peace Prayer" of Francis of Assisi has attained, like the saint himself, multicultural and interreligious prominence: "Lord, make me an instrument..." In it, the asker requests simply that he or she be a channel of peace, love, pardon, joy, consolation, understanding—all these fine and splendid things we associate with God and the state of grace.

The prayer, with all its broad appeal, is quintessentially Christian. It is founded on the belief that the Creator-God, the loving Father-God, has indeed acted in and through the human we hail as Christ. It expresses the continued conviction that the Trinity indwells the human person and that the Spirit, whom John Paul II says *is* "personal love," is manifest in our transitory lives.

What is a source of awe and humility is our discovery time and again, if we have opened ourselves, that God can use us as instruments in spite of our shortcomings, in spite of our errors, in spite of our sins. Somehow we speak a word that encourages. Somehow we make the helpful suggestion. Somehow we affirm and reassure. Somehow we simply appear in the right place at the right moment or make the very timely phone call. Someone tells us what we once did or said made a tremendous difference, and we find that we have no memory of ever having expressed such thoughts or sentiments, no recollection of having done the deed.

God works.

And God's love flows through all of us, it seems, if we give love even the smallest aperture through our being. We duplicate, even in our malaprop, semi-aware way, that experience of Jesus:

the being sent, the divine companionship, the doing of God's pleasure.

God takes us, no matter how world-weary we are, no matter how unequipped, no matter how sullied, at our sincere word: "Lord, make me an instrument...."

Lord, my self-offering is often halfhearted, and yet I mean to be someone through whom light shines and love exudes. Make me a channel, Lord, of you.

WEDNESDAY OF THE FIFTH WEEK
John 8:31–42

Jesus answered them, "Very truly I tell you, everyone who commits sin is a slave to sin." John 8:34

In his book *Sin as Addiction*, Patrick McCormick treats sin as an orientation of one's character to flawed or vicious ends. Sin is comparable to sickness, McCormick argues, because in sin people "experience themselves as disoriented, weakened and impaired." Sin is also comparable to addiction, because, unlike the sickness that comes upon one involuntarily, and often apart from any question of personal responsibility, sin is something that involves the "whole person." In the beginning, at least, there is some free choice. But sin also, when understood as state and habit, entails a gradual loss of freedom—as self-deception, denial, moral breakdown, dependency, self-obsession, distorted relations with others, disrupted control and dissociation from feeling increasingly rule the person's thoughts and behaviors.

Sin, according to Anne Wilson Schaef, is "anything you need to lie about." Thus, sin serves as a good description not only of those personal things we would prefer to keep hidden or masqueraded, but also those large-scale societal things we support under other guises: things like consumerism and militarism, for example. We might add, in America, racism and violence, both of which rear up in more subtle forms in our language and jokes and in more evident forms in our choices for entertainment as well as in our oft-reported crimes.

None of us likes to fancy ourselves slaves to anything. Yet we persist in our fixations about what people think; we try to please one and all; we gossip; we dull our sensibilities with TV watching; we overeat; we shop compulsively; we avoid self-scrutiny by keeping busy. We also prefer not to reflect on how our comforts, our suburban escapes, our vacation spots, and our fast-food establishments implicate us in the discomfort of the world's poor and the degradation of both human culture and Earth's environment.

Perhaps to locate where our true sin lies we have only to ask ourselves what it is that we could not bear to live without.

What (to ask the 12-step questions) is it that has power over us to the extent that we are incapable of seizing power over it?

We may make some distressing personal and societal discoveries.

Give me freedom, God, to face my unfreedoms squarely. And give me power to turn my life over to you, the Higher Power, for the liberating effects of your grace.

THURSDAY OF THE FIFTH WEEK
John 8:51–59

"Your ancestor Abraham rejoiced that he would see my day; he saw it and was glad."   John 8:56

How do we possibly see a day—the "day of the Lord" or even some lesser yet long-awaited day—if we don't actually have physical evidence of it? How does a Dr. Martin Luther King, Jr., see the day when the descendants of slaveholders and the descendants of slaves work side by side and walk hand-in-hand? How does a Dorothy Day see the time when the poor will be housed and fed and when nations will disarm their warheads? How does an Abraham see a day when God will speak not only from the sky, not only in an old man's heart, not only in an angel who stays a would-be slayer's hand, but with a human voice, a voice that can comfort, preach, demand, and cry out in pain? How do we see a day when the "reign of God," a reign of justice and truth and mercy and love, will come in fullness?

It is a matter of hope. It is also a gift of imagining. All of us are equipped not only with the framework of time and space and the limits of our mental and physical capacities but also with the capacity to dream, to foresee, and to enter at moments into the transcendent. We humans have inklings (and more) that we surpass our own mortality. We have, as the wise might say, *capax universi:* a capacity for the universe.

If we are attentive, if we watch closely, if we stay at prayer, we can begin to observe the irreversible trends of history, including, of course, the history of human salvation. If we walk by faith, we can notice, too, the irresistible tendencies of grace.

That is what, Jesus appears to say, made for Abraham's story and the way that he "rejoiced that he would see my day."

That attentiveness too, that persistence in faith, is what made it possible for the disciples in the upper room to wait for the coming of the Spirit and then to go forth to proclaim the resurrection that still is.

That hopeful, prayerful imagining is what allows us, too, to anticipate a day of glory, a day when all creation will be embraced in Light.

As I meditate, as I sit still and wait, let me see, dear

God, beyond this day. Let me know the goal of glory and move me to do whatever is my part in bringing about your reign in human hearts.

FRIDAY OF THE FIFTH WEEK
John 10:31–42

Jesus answered, "Is it not written in your law, 'I said, you are gods'? If those to whom the word of God came were called 'gods'—and the scripture cannot be annulled—can you say that the one whom the Father has sanctified and sent into the world is blaspheming?" *John 10:34-36*

Jesus often expressed a shocking familiarity with God. And he often made claims not only about himself but also about the host of ordinary humans and even the outcast, which seemed to exceed the bounds of humility.

He let it be known that he was anointed of God, God's very son. He announced that all the common-born who were bonded to him were also the apple of God's eye, God's heirs, God's pride and joy, God's chosen and children. He equated love of the neighbor with, and subsumed human love within, the love of God. He warned that the measure of our moral lives would be our treatment of the "least," the neediest, and that such would be deemed equivalent to our treatment of him, the Messiah, the holy one of God.

Though he offered "signs," the "works of my father" that he performed on an everyday basis, none such were really needed. The persuasive startlement of his faith in the human, his reverence for the dissolute and "unclean," gave testimony that ought to have been quite enough that Jesus himself bore the heart of God.

The word of God, Jesus reminds his hearers, called the hearers of the word "gods." In the fourth century of this era, St. Athanasius declared, "If the works of the Logos's Godhead had not been done by means of the body, humanity would not have been divinized." This divinization, the deification of the human, is a theme that pervades the Eastern Christian tradition. It refers to what it means, ultimately, to be sanctified: to be *at* one and *as* one with God.

In the twentieth century, Karl Rahner has observed: "We may safely say that with a communion of brothers and sisters, in its necessary oneness with the love of God, we have expressed the single totality of the task of the whole human being and of Christianity" (*The Love of Jesus and the Love of Neighbor*). This requires of us not just a personal charity but a "political theology," Rahner says, and an active concern for the "anonymous crowd" of worldwide humanity.

If we take the words of Jesus and the reflections of master theologians to heart, we begin to realize that every human being merits the reverential bow, the tender treatment, that we reserve for the sacred. Christianity at its core declares that every Christian must genuflect before the other and have the same sort of quiet awe that he or she holds before the tabernacle. We *must*, the gospel teaches, treat the other, no matter who, as "host," as Body of Christ, as God of Life.

We are so little accustomed to acting or thinking in such a way, though, that the idea seems a trivialization of God, a blasphemy.

Meanwhile the breadth, the widespreadness, of godliness is simply the manifestation of God's own grandiosity.

Lord, deepen my reverence, my awe, my tenderness. I need not look far to catch sight of you. You are sister, brother, neighbor, earthling, even as you are more.

SATURDAY OF THE FIFTH WEEK
John 11:45–57

So the chief priests and the Pharisees called a meeting of the council, and said, "What are we to do? This man is performing many signs. If we let him go on like this, everyone will believe in him, and the Romans will come and destroy both our holy place and our nation."

John 11:47-48

If we listen too closely to environmentalists or Third World theologians, let's say, we stand in grave danger. Our very life-styles and our institutions stand under threat. When Worldwatch reports the state of forests, waters, air, and soils, the only logical thing to conclude is that we must vastly alter the way we build, dispose of waste, run our industries, plant our crops, and coax our lawns to grow. But to do otherwise than we currently do would cost us jobs, shops, stock dividends. When Jon Sobrino of El Salvador publicly attacks the capital sin of greed and the monetary root of evil, it begins to seem that parishes ought to raise funds differently, that dioceses could spend their resources better than they do, that Catholic colleges and universities ought not so unquestioningly to accept grants and endowments from businesses and government and industry or student benefits from R.O.T.C. But to get down and dirty at that level of questioning could undo the whole hierarchical and educational fabric.

Jesus was a threat not merely because of his charismatic personality and his popularity with lowlife types, but because his teachings rocked the foundations of religion and society. His testimony suggested, as did that of the prophets of old, that the only sure way to God was a way of massive redirection. As some anonymous wag has had it, one of the spiritual works of mercy is to comfort the afflicted, but one of the works of Jesus seems to be to afflict the comfortable.

The scribes and the Pharisees fear Jesus because he challenges their axioms and their way of life. He is also a threat to the sanctuary and the law. His refusal to pay any particular attention to ritual purity, his hobnobbing with the sinners and the not strictly observant, his preference for the oppressed, his casual descriptions of his "Father" and of the way of holiness—these unstrung all those who were sure that the way of righteousness was doing all the right things via the right prescriptions and having a distanced, somewhat tremulous, very pious regard for God. One ought not even breathe God's proper name.

But the holy ones also feared Jesus because he did indeed seem to provoke division. Any show of something less than tight Jewish solidarity threatened to bring down the thunder of Rome on the people. An internal power struggle, signs of local strife, could, they were sure, render them more vulnerable. And all would be lost.

The scribes and Pharisees are entirely too much like us. We would prefer a religion of security and sure things. We would prefer a preaching that does not disrupt the status quo. We would prefer a religion that has no internal disputes and in which all are blithely cooperative, compliant, and comfortable.

Anyone who proffers too many unpleasant facts or poses any profoundly unsettling questions may require us to rethink and, worse yet, reconstruct our lives and our practice from the bottom up.

It is far easier to silence the prophets and banish the agitators and leave it to later ages to canonize them. We then can die in our air-conditioning, be buried in our plush caskets, and have a nice quiet requiem in our newly renovated chapels.

God forbid that I respond to the prophetic voice with a resounding "Drop dead!" Yet there are many fronts on which I wish not to be met or moved. Afflict my comforts, Lord, where it will do the most good.

PASSION (PALM) SUNDAY
YEAR A Matthew 26:14—27:66 • YEAR B Mark 14:1—15:47
YEAR C Luke 22:14—23:56

Then the people as a whole answered, "His blood be on us and on our children!" Matthew 27:25

There is something altogether disconcerting, when the Passion is read with multiple voices, about finding that we in the pews have to take the part of the rabble. The mass of the congregation has to join chorus and declare "Barabbas!" as our choice. We accuse Peter, surmising his associations by his accent. We say things of Jesus: "We found this man perverting our nation." Or, mockingly, "He saved others; he cannot save himself." And we hurl insults at Jesus: "Prophesy! Who is it that struck you?" We raise the chilling outcry, "Crucify him!" And then we taunt, "Let the Messiah, the king of Israel, come down from the cross now, so that we may see and believe."

Of course, it is only an act. We assume the voices for the sake of drama. That, at least, is what we like to think.

Yet every day, sadly, we hear reports of domestic violence and family mayhem. Relatives turn on those who ought most to have loved them—and perhaps in some way have. We read of still another lawsuit, brought by a beneficiary against a benefactor, a person who lent a hand, gave a ride, rushed to assist in some mishap. We awaken to the news that a peacemaker has been taken hostage or shot on the way to a presidential palace or that a promising student leader has been felled in a spray of gang bullets.

We cannot condone such things. We would never, we insist, participate in them.

Yet we bypass the reminders of our spoiled friendships and loves. We harbor resentment against the professor who questioned our capability or the physician who could not mend our twisted bones or kill our recurrent pain. We are angry at the government, the military, business, industry, the hierarchy of the church, and the times.

We refuse to ask ourselves how a siege of Leningrad, a Nazi holocaust, an atomic slaughter of Japanese, a blight of disappearances and torture in Latin America, government-sponsored executions, apartheid in South Africa, raging homelessness in America, a dismaying escalation of crime, and abortions in the millions could happen in this century.

We kill our kin and grow callous to innocence. Can it really surprise us that our race has nailed and spit at God?

Quiet me, God, that I may hear. Hold up for me a mirror that I may see my face before it turns to mob.

MONDAY OF HOLY WEEK
John 12:1–11

Mary took a pound of costly perfume made of pure nard, anointed Jesus' feet, and wiped them with her hair. The house was filled with the fragrance of perfume.   *John 12:3*

The fragrance of a good cure fills the house; the fragrance of a fine therapy permeates the persons in the rooms. The fragrance of tender caring that throws itself at the feet of the one who needs soothing: this fragrance spreads and filters through. Sometimes it seems to fill the world.

There is a strangeness to having one's feet washed and wiped with someone's hair. But there is a strangeness, too, come to think of it, in being served tea and crackers amid nausea, in having cool cloths brought for one's fever, in being fed and talked to when one can do nothing but lie in a hospital bed in blankness, in being held when one is sweating with AIDS.

In the midst of a world whose terrorism, crime, abuse, neglect, hate are well publicized, it is still possible to find extravagances of love.

When we receive them in our illness, loneliness, distress, or fear, we can only conclude that these extravagances come from much love. They shore us up and help us face death. They remind us that there are still people who love other people, even love us, as if we were the Incarnate God.

> Dear God, when I am the receiver of someone else's acts of caring, and even of someone's excesses, help me to recall their origin in the divinest love. Let the aroma of kindness, of every single strange and gentle deed, fill our human space like a lavishness of nard.

TUESDAY OF HOLY WEEK
John 13:21–33, 36–38

> After saying this, Jesus was troubled in spirit and declared, "Very truly, I tell you, one of you will betray me." John 13:21

It seems, unfortunately, that every human being can identify with the feelings that accompany betrayal: the stun of recognition, the "deeply troubled" spirit, the helplessness, the foreboding, the wish to get things over with. In ways great or small, all of us have been disappointed, dumbfounded by disappearances, dismayed when our best efforts have seemed suddenly but surely undone.

Judas moved from petty thievery to gross sellout. Simon swore undying loyalty to the man he not so much later denied. And a crowd echoing hosannas began the murmur that moved to outcry and bloodbath: "Crucify!"

How is it that romance fades, love becomes amnesiac, once-faithful friends turn opponent, and the well-laid plans for grace and benefit go all awry? How is it that promises turn to walkout and even crime? How does day, out of sync and out of season, eclipse so abruptly to night?

When we feel denied and betrayed, it can seem a rather small comfort to recall that God understands. Betrayal still, after all, stays unfixed and stings beyond bearing. And when we ourselves have betrayed—which we so easily do when it seems that life is holding a gun to our heads—we can hardly help but feel like devils.

At the very least, we weep. Betrayed or betraying, denied or denying, we pain because it seems so clear that there is no way to rewind, no way to brush out the traces of our footsteps, no way to cram back into our throats the fatal words, no way to restrain the deadening deeds. Some harm cannot be reversed. Some harm sets a course.

The only consolation, God knows, is that the betrayal and harm we have endured or have inflicted may be remade somehow—amid almighty mystery—into glory. That glory does not erase guilt. But it does instill hope that the words of Paul to the Romans still ring true: that all things can actually "work to good."

God of majesty and triumph, turn the harms I have done and the harms done to me into something that transforms, into something that changes course, into something that makes for maturity and growth. I do not wish to minimize the evil we humans do, the denials we make, but I want to hope that you can overcome the sin and the mistake.

WEDNESDAY OF HOLY WEEK
Matthew 26:14–25

He answered, "The one who has dipped his hand into the bowl with me will betray me."   Matthew 26:23

Betrayal by friends, family, associates is one thing. Another is betrayal by the elements themselves—the land that slides, the planet that quakes, the storms that erode beach or drown crops, the rivers that flood a broader plain than ever before, the tornado that suctions up unaccountably. There ought to be, we feel, some range of predictability. There ought to be some way for us to live in harmony with land and sea and air, to revere their power, and to protect ourselves so that we don't find ourselves done violence by them.

Then there is the betrayal by our bodies. Accident victims, the aging, the acutely stricken feel this betrayal. Whether the consequence of wear and years or surprise attack, illness and handicap leave us in disarray. The permanently disabled and the chronically ill feel—understandably—chronically, permanently victimized.

When all of our best efforts have gone into conforming to regimens of medication, diet, exercise, preventive care, all sorts of therapies, it is hard to feel anything but betrayed when these efforts seem ineffective. There seems to be a failure of medicine and the body to interact. The promising surgery doesn't correct our vision; the lasers don't quite smash the stones; the new knee doesn't remedy our gimpy walk; the recombinant DNA insulin still doesn't get the sugar under optimum control; the painkiller reputed to have minimal adverse effects fails to still our pain while it succeeds at adversely affecting us; the antibiotic supposed to quell our infection meets a new resistant bacterial strain, and infected we remain. We feel betrayed by human finitude: our own mortality and vulnerability; the limits of medical know-how;

the intricacies of our own biochemical, organic, orthopedic complexities.

There is some point at which surrender is called for—by life and by God. Calamities of nature, freak accidents, and the wily ways of human flesh and bone can't be attributed to any malice. Tsunamis and falls down the stairs, hurricanes and arthritis and a genetic predisposition to multiple sclerosis really can't be regarded as Judases. Yet there comes a point at which we must name them, acknowledge the enemy, dip into the dish, and then go on. There is, it seems, some sort of "appointed time" in every life. There are circumstances that rush headlong to their logical conclusions. Some suppers run relentlessly into arrests and deaths.

The question is how to know when to resist and when just to submit to whatever unfolds. How do we know what sort of Sunday morning aftermath may be hidden within the undoings or betrayals that afflicts us?

Dear Lord, I tend to feel that life itself sometimes betrays me. Give me whatever strength and resourcefulness I need to resist the wear and tear of affliction. But also give me the gentleness of spirit to know when to give in and go along. Help me to live in harmony with nature itself and with the nature of my fragility.

HOLY THURSDAY
John 13:1–15

"I have set you an example, that you also should do as I have done to you."   John 13:15

When Aunt Mary and Uncle Les were already in their eighties, she joked about the operation of putting his support socks on in the morning. She had to kneel on the floor and pull. She spoke of it as "paying homage" to Uncle Les and teasingly called him "M'lord."

When Martin Luther reflected on parenthood and the sacred trust which children are, he concluded that fathers ought to change diapers. He wrote, more than four centuries ago: "When a father goes ahead and washes diapers or performs some other mean task for his child, and someone ridicules him as an effeminate fool...God, with all his angels and creatures, is smiling—not because that father is washing diapers, but because he is doing so in Christian faith." The child, Luther is sure, is a blessed work of God.

The care of humans by other humans is often menial, sometimes messy. There can be a kind of ridiculousness about it.

In the time of Jesus, washing the road dust and desert sand from rough, sandaled feet was the job of self or slaves, mothers or maidservants. The one who washed for the other showed a certain deference, a certain homage, to the one whose feet were being washed.

Thus, the sight of Jesus, the master and rabbi—the Messiah, too, some also believed—washing feet was something of a shock.

His message is also something of a shock: "So if I, your Lord and Teacher, have washed your feet, you also ought to wash one another's feet" (John 13:14). Once again we hear that the human person is worthy of the deference we give to "superiors" and even the reverence we owe to God.

If we are holy, we understand that there is every reason to wash feet, pull on socks, clean up wounds and messes, change and wash diapers.

Mother Teresa of Calcutta has said, in telling the story of a man who lay rotting and dying in a sewer drain and was found covered with maggots, that pulling the maggots off him, cleansing his sores, and soothing the man were acts done to and for the Body of Christ. It is not as if her imagination somehow superimposed Christ on the wretched, wracked man. It is that the man himself, in his fatal misery, and the Christ were one and the same.

Those of us who spend Holy Thursday kneeling before an exposed Blessed Sacrament need to recall that Jesus would also have us kneeling reverently before one another.

Lord, give me eyes to see and the heart to know that you are real and present before me—in persons, in grime, in the one who needs me to do. Give me the spirit of true homage and deference.

GOOD FRIDAY
John 18:1–19, 42

Then he handed him over to them to be crucified.
John 19:16

One of the journalistic coups of the second half of the twentieth century was *Time* magazine's presenting, just in time for Good Friday 1966, an issue that carried a black cover imprinted with the red letters of these three words: Is God Dead?

The cover story identified the "death of God" theologians, the theologians of "non-theology," as Thomas J. J. Altizer, William Hamilton, and Paul Van Buren. It related them to, and in a sense grounded them in, Nietzsche—in his "thesis" that "striving, self-centered man had killed God." For illustrations of the theological and religious tug-of-war, the magazine's editors juxtaposed, in facing pages, photos of the great Manhattan blackout and a painting of an old, white, heavily browed and bearded God by Raphael; a delivery room in Seattle with smiling mother and squawking newborn and the flattened, lifeless specter that was the rubble of Hiroshima; an El Greco Resurrection and an ad for an astonishing new "computyper." Aside from providing an exposition of the latest ditherings of academics, the story displayed the indefinability of God as person or concept—and the dismaying evidence of God's irrelevance to a world gone secular.

Some thirty years later, religion has endured many controversies and many alterations but not a demise. Majorities in repeated polls claim to believe in a God of some sort and say they invoke that God at times in prayer. Yet it would seem, even to the casual observer, that what *Time* observed in 1966 is still abundantly around: the phenomenon of "practical atheism." Churchgoing happens, people profess to believe, but "faith" is a kind of compartment of life that doesn't intersect with much that goes on during the workaday week.

Perhaps the most urgent question for a Good Friday is not "Were You There...?" as the old hymn asks, but rather this one: Have we killed, are we still killing, God?

There is evidence that we have.

The Christ was crucified because of duplicity, complacency, resistance to change, refusal to see and hear, fear, unwillingness to endure threats to security and comfort.

We who are living the transition to the third millennium of Christianity seem similarly afflicted. We First Worlders in particular are preoccupied with our properties, our incomes, our gadgets, our retirement plans, our diets, our vacations, our transit systems, our communications networks, our clothes, our colleges, our medical plans, our speed, our psyches, our overload. If we can hardly see constellations for the glitter of our cities, if we can hardly catch sight of honeysuckle and brown-eyed susans as we whizz by on our interstates, we should hardly be surprised that we can't quite focus on or relate to the idea of a Creator. If we have schooled ourselves well in averting our eyes from the tattered sitter on the sidewalk and the bulbous-bellied Third World child covered with flies, if we have learned that even our best loves don't last and are convinced that those who disappoint us should be cast off, we should hardly be astonished that a God in human form, a crucified one at that, strikes us as incomprehensible. If we have become unable to sit silently and still amid rock garden and night dew, if we have grown unattuned to the whisper of wisdom and the murmurings of conscience, we should hardly think it shocking to find that the Holy Spirit seems as phantasmagoric and cartoonish as the poltergeists and ghosts featured in Hollywood videos.

We have killed God, we are killing God, wherever we crowd God out. We deal God a death blow when we decline to call a halt and contemplate. We deliver God's post-mortem when we turn from the living field, the living stream, the stalwart deer, the longing human being and notice nothing intrinsically good, inherently valuable, invincibly holy in all of these. We bury God when all that we embrace is a drink, a steering wheel, an investment package, another fleeting fad and fanfare.

Disclose, Lord, the spirit of assault that dwells in me. Drive from me whatever would violate all that lives, all that has being. Make me reverent, attentive, and alive to your living.

HOLY SATURDAY

John Cage, the experimental composer and conductor, attained notoriety for such musical shenanigans as Quartet for Twelve Tom-Toms and Radio Music, which of course turned out differently each time, since it required artists to twist dials and depend on the unpredictable programming of the radio stations in any locale where the piece was performed.

Cage also alternately intrigued and outraged listeners and concertgoers by the insertion of extended dead spaces—long, long rests—into his symphonies and concerti. He wanted listeners to become aware of what lay in between the impact of sound waves. Silence was, he believed, dynamic and pregnant, filled with suspense.

The church on Holy Saturday forces silence upon us. It is the one day of the liturgical year for which there is no Eucharistic celebration. If one happens by the parish church before the array of lilies and candles are reinstated in preparation for the Vigil Mass, one finds the altar stripped, the tabernacle door open, the sanctuary lamp quenched. The stark and barren decor—or, actually, the lack of decor at all—are meant to reflect the long pause, the noiselessness of the unknown.

The length of hours between Good Friday when Jesus cried "It is finished!" and the dawnlight of Easter is time that has been muted and killed.

It is an uneasy silence that recalls that once there were stunned and stock-still disciples who did not know whether that silence would ever be broken.

God of long wait and wonderment, attune my listening heart so that I can detect the earliest soundings of good news. Help me, too, to wait things through in quiet, with you.

EASTER VIGIL
YEAR A Matthew 28:1–10 • YEAR B Mark 16:1–8
YEAR C Luke 24:1–12

"He has been raised; he is not here. Look, there is the
place they laid him. But go, tell his disciples..."

Mark 16:6-7

In the end, we find that Christianity is a comic rather than a tragic religion.

We continue to bollix things up. Mark says that the women
who went to the tomb and found that Jesus had risen were too
afraid to tell anyone, even though they were supposed to.
Matthew and Luke can't agree on whether one angel or two were
hanging about the tomb that morning. There is fear and confusion and incomprehension.

What makes Christianity comic is that all the bungling is overcome. The resurrection is proclaimed. Witnesses add to the
accounts and give their testimony. The gospel is preached. The
church is born.

The resurrection of Jesus communicates the very *un*tragic message, the very glorious and hope-filled truth: the power of hatred
and the power of wrongful death can be and are undone. The end
of the story is not, as in Shakespeare's *Hamlet,* unmitigated disas-
ter. The tales of Jesus do not end with a desolate stage and a body
count.

Jesus is, instead, found to be among "the living" (Luke 24:5).
Neither devils nor our whole human race can prevent him from
meeting us in Galilee and seeing us again.

Jesus, Rabboni, greet me with your peace. Dispel all my
dreads with confidence, and let "alleluia!" vibrate from
me, head to toe, heaven to good Earth. Amen. And again,
Amen.

EASTER EVER AFTER:
A PERSONAL MEMOIR

There are days when I feel particularly useless and bleak. I question whether anything I have ever said or done has made any sense or served any purpose. I wander the city streets or drive blank countryside wishing for something to stir me. I daze into daydream and then stop dead, sure that my imaginings are wayward and a waste. I wonder if those of us who have staked their lives on God might awake one day and find it all smoke and delusion. I ask if those of us who have tried to serve in some altruistic way might not just as well have been scalpers, madams, Mafiosi. And I struggle to understand what makes it possible to have friends and loves and living kin and still feel abysmally abandoned and alone. How is it that belief in our minds and consent in our wills can't seem to make it through to our nervous systems and our clanging emotions? I lament my medical battles and my lifelong lack of time and funds.

On such a day, on Fifth Avenue in Pittsburgh, I once watched a man with a white cane stumble up a curb and walk straight for a mailbox. Passersby rushing to offices or buses dodged him, embarrassed. I decided to catch up as I saw him begin to trip again and head toward a low cement wall. I took hold of his elbow, and then we shifted so that he could take hold of my arm, as blind people do.

His name was Terry. He had graduated in the late 1970s from the same university where I was teaching in the mid-1990s. He had come from his home in Penn Hills, he explained, and somehow the driver had let him off a block too far from his destination. It had disoriented him, broken the stride of his measured pacings. And it was wildly raining, so sounds were distorted and awash.

He told me which of the string of buildings in the Pitt Medical Center he was to go to. His appointment was on the fifth floor. In the lobby, though he had been there before, he still seemed a bit confused. Perhaps the University of Pittsburgh, an everlasting reconfigurer and remodeler of its buildings, had changed it since the last time. Whatever the problem was, I told him I'd go upstairs with him.

As we exited the elevator, I found it impossible to imagine how he would have ever, on his own, located the receptionist. The office was tucked away around a maze of corners and bends. Even with sight, I found the route almost indecipherable. There was no human being, no one adept at directions or otherwise, anywhere near the elevators, and there were no signs.

When we finally found the receptionist by trial and error, Terry checked in. He would be maneuvered around from there on, I was assured. It was my turn to leave.

If it does anything, I mused, perhaps Christianity predisposes one to think that it's reasonable to halt another aimless traipsing of the city and accompany an off-course blind man to an appointment. Perhaps the gospel of neighbor-love sets off a small alarm in one's head that alerts one to do something other than gawk at a stumbling man who's lost.

If I were ever blind, I said to myself, I would hope that someone would stop and introduce himself or herself and walk with me.

So, I had said it!

Blindness is something I would rather not think about at all. As a diabetic who already shows some traces of retinopathy, the odds are that my vision will not hold out lifelong. The blood vessels of the retina begin to explode, and premature cataracts are also an all too likely hazard. I use my vision all day long, so the very thought of impairment is dismaying. I would rather, I have often thought, go deaf than lose my sight, even though deaf people have told me that they would rather be blind. When I consider blindness at all, it makes me quite wild and agonized.

But then there was Terry, an exceedingly gentle and patient man. He readily accepted my arm and trusted my voice. Though

I have never met him again, I have been touched by him in a way that defies explanation. I would readily have gone home with him if that had seemed appropriate. Perhaps I would have caught some of Terry's calm.

I have friends who have wanted to conceal themselves in the hollows of trees and friends who have wanted to flee the madding crowd and live on grubs and wild berries and old bread crusts in hidden caves. I have met a blind man who walked into my heart and showed me that perhaps one need not flee life.

My religion believes that trees and caves have self-surpassing significance. They are intimately linked to paschal mystery.

My religion also teaches that the desolate and self-absorbed can awake to another, even to someone they have never come upon before. And the church is sure that the blind can see.

It believes in a Christ who smacks into mailboxes across the centuries. It believes in a treed man, waked in a cave, who continues to speak in a kindly voice despite the hazards of Fifth Avenues and fifth floors.

Of Related Interest...

40 Days of Grace
Lenten Prayers and Reflections
Laurin J. Wenig

These insightful reflections lead readers into a meaningful
lenten experience of renewal.
ISBN: 0-89622-665-4, 176 pp, $9.95 (order M-56)

The Parables of Calvary
Reflections on the Seven Last Words of Jesus
Stephen C. Rowan

A unique book! The author compares the last words
of Jesus on the cross with his parables and opens up
the rich meanings that affect our lives. A lovely book
for all seasons.
ISBN: 0-89622-576-3, 56 pp, $4.95 (order B-77)

Still on the Cross
*Meditations on the Human Condition
and the Desperate Passion of Jesus*
Loretta Girzaitis & Richard L. Wood

This book links the passion of Christ with contemporary
injustice and highlights the Christian mission to continue Christ's saving work.
ISBN: 0-89622-449-X, 80 pp, $5.95 (order W-32)

Available at religious bookstores or from:

XXIII **TWENTY-THIRD PUBLICATIONS**
P.O. Box 180 • Mystic, CT 06355

For a complete list of quality books and videos call:
1 - 8 0 0 - 3 2 1 - 0 4 1 1